SANATAN KRIYA
51 MIRACLES...
...and a haunting

YOGI ASHWINI

Published by

Dhyan Foundation
A-80, South Extension-II, New Delhi
website: www.dhyanfoundation.com
e-mail: dhyan@dhyanfoundation.com.

Printed in India by

Niyogi Offset Pvt. Ltd.

Rs. 500.00

ISBN 978-81-904506-4-5

foreword

A distraught mother sees a steel wire nearly decapitate her teenaged daughter. The doctors are not sure if she would live, but they are sure that even if she does, she would definitely not be able to speak ever again; and yet, today that girl is not only alive and speaking, but is also heard chanting. The doctors can't believe their ears. "It's a miracle", they say...

A woman is exploring a cave in Austria. The ground is slippery and drops away at a steep angle into a nearby gorge. The woman trips... The other tourists in the cave raise an alarm but can do little as they helplessly watch her as she slides along the icy floor towards the bottomless gorge. She closes her eyes and prays for deliverance. She sees the hand of her Guru... She says, "It cant be in my imagination because I held it and it saved my life! My family and friends are a testimony to it." Those who saw her fall in that cave can't believe she survived without a scratch. Yet again, "It's a miracle!" they say....

> He is very much in the body and alive and living with us. He is not a story, He is not a myth and He is not history...He is here and now and He is for real.

A Dhyan Foundation publication, Sanatan Kriya: 51 Miracles... is their story and the story of 49 others who have been touched by life-changing miracles. These miracles are not just possible "but it is impossible for them not to happen, if you walk on the path of Yog and have the *sanidhya* of a Guru", says Yogi Ashwini, the leading light of Dhyan Foundation.

In a world that has learnt to reward scepticism and accept pessimism, this book gives reasons for hope, and gently, but firmly, pushes us awake from our sleep to a world of magical possibilities that had existed all around us and yet until nudged awake, we had slept through our lives, oblivious to its divine and enchanted existence. This book is that wake up call...

I have grown up listening to stories on miracles, I have read many books on them too. The lacuna has always been that these masters are no more in their bodies, and neither are those people who have experienced these miracles. So the logical mind remains thirsty for the lack of validations and self-experience. This book fills up that gap... In this day and age, it is truly amazing to be able to meet in flesh and blood such a yogi and actually experience His abilities, of course with 51 validations, for the logical mind.

This book not only tells us about a living master but actually makes us experience Him through the medium of the contributors. The solace here is that He is very much in the body and alive and living with us. He is not a story, He is not a myth and He is not history…He is here and now and He is for real.

I now invite you to enter this world of miracles… and a haunting.

Prashanto Banerjee
Features Editor, Sunday Indian

preface

This book is not written for the believer, for the believer should have had the desired experience of the subtle world by now. The believer should have found a Guru by now and should already be immersed in the nectar that is SHIV and SHIVA. The believer need not read any more, for the believer already knows... whatever there is to be known.

You might have read a lot of books on Yoga. You might have memorised many *sutras* and *shlokas* and perhaps by now have emptied your bank accounts paying fees for the various courses offered on spirituality. And yet, if 'the experience' has evaded you till now, and if you meditate and your mind opens up to forceful visualisations; if you imagine various things and try to see them or if you are trying to reach there by breathing rather abnormally or by tying yourself up in knots or even trying to learn some forms of engineering, and calling it Yoga, then you can be sure that you are not 'a believer'. All you have is knowledge and you are forcing your mind to show you things. You are actually operating within the seven to eight per cent of your mind's capacity that is suited only for the functioning of your five senses, keeping the balance 92 per cent unutilised, and as Swami Satyananda says, "You are day dreaming." You are increasing just plain and simple knowledge, just like a computer's hard drive, which has it all, yet has experienced nothing; for it lacks the experience, *GYAN* and of course, the grace of the GURU. This 92 per cent is something that only your Guru can open for you, and to open this, he/she would first need to take you through the dual process of *KAYA STHIRAM* followed by *TATTWA GYAN*, and then give you *SHAKTIPATH*. It is only then that the unutilised chambers of your brain would open and the secrets of Creation would be revealed to you. You would be a *GYANI* and a YOGI.

Till you actually receive the *GYAN* through a GURU, THE MIRACLE shall evade you. *SHIVO HUM* shall remain a distant dream... and you will still go around searching for new books on yoga and the paranormal, and for teachers and masters.

I can actually afford to talk about what I have written above, for till around 15 years back, I was just like this - an ordinary seeker, and a regular at classes on various aspects of the world of the paranormal and forms of energy healing, or various forms of neo-yoga, a couple of which I found were teaching diverse aspects of the arts of living (please don't waste my time, I am looking for something beyond living). I asked myself, 'What's all this? Everyone here seems to want something from me? Either my money as fee or my time to help build them up! Does a spiritual quest not take you beyond the clutches of physical attractions? Why is everyone talking about healing the body and having more fun in the realm of the physical world?' My experiences led me to believe that actually, I was running on a treadmill. Yes, I was happy and enjoying myself to the hilt... but, I had not moved forward even by an inch! Actually, I concluded that clubbing openly and partying was a much better option. At least in that case I would have been truthful to myself... and to GOD.

Then 'the Miracle' happened! I met my GURU, and to that energy I dedicate this book, for its only because of that energy, that in the last seven years or so, volunteers at Dhyan Foundation

> A miracle is actually a fact of nature which is beyond the capacity of the normal mind to interpret. As you grow in yoga, miracles become a way of life for you...

have experienced more than 500 miracles; whether it is to do with a medical problem, a past-life experience, a brush with the world of the occult and black magic, or an interaction with the subtler dimensions where ancient texts have been revealed.

I actually wanted to write a series of books on MIRACLES but my GURU gave me permission for publishing only 51 such miracles and one haunting account. The clear instruction was that the purpose of this book is simply to tell the 'World' that there really is something 'beyond'... and if one would not believe it after reading about it in 51 ways, then one first needs to learn the art of living it up here in any up-market nightclub and only then come to the Dhyan Foundation for a journey beyond. In the words of my GURU, "A miracle is actually a fact of nature which is beyond the capacity of the normal mind to interpret. As you grow in yoga, miracles become a way of life for you... But then for you they are not miracles anymore but simple laws of nature that you now understand and use for aiding the positive forces of Creation to make this world a happy place to be in, and in the process, you too go beyond.

I invite the reader to go through these 51 miracles and welcome any investigation with respect to their authenticity. All the subjects are very much here and open to interviews and scrutiny of medical records or testimonies of friends and relatives. The only thing that I would not be able to prove to the investigator would be the past lives of the subjects, as their knowledge stems from my thought and to empirically see that, you have to access me through the path of the *GURU SHISHYA PARAMPARA*.

Yogi Ashwini

a note

Each one at Dhyan Foundation is a living testimony to the miraculous effects of Sanatan Kriya and the ability and power of a Yog Guru.

Every miracle in this book is a personal and individual account, and a tribute to the Grace of the Guru. However, these miracles are not a substitute for the medical science, but indicate a world that extends beyond...

It should be noted that this book is not an attempt to discourage the reader from visiting a doctor when need arises, but a window to the truly miraculous world of Yog and Sanatan Kriya.

We invite you to not only read someone else's miracles, but to also do your own practice of Sanatan Kriya and experience for yourself the truths of the inner world.

Yogi Ashwini says,

"If you are sick, go to the doctor, don't come to me.
If you want to experience the subtler worlds,
don't go to the doctor, come to me."

DHYAN FOUNDATION

contents

51 miracles...

51 miracles...

01 the sound of silence

GURUSPEAK

Abha, like every other mother, was extremely concerned about her daughter's health. She was completely disappointed with the medical community, not because medical science is without value, but because medical science can only comprehend what physical instruments can interpret, what the five senses can perceive. But then there are matters which these instruments don't reveal and which the five senses don't perceive. Just like a little time lock, for instance. Gravity or the layers to the atmosphere, one would not have accepted, but now since instruments can measure them and the senses can feel them, so we accept them. Similarly, the subtler layers to physically manifested Creation, which are not perceivable to modern instruments and presently activated senses, would one day be perceivable to man, as they were perceivable to Vedic ***rishis*** *and are perceivable to ...GURUS.*

Her extraordinary faith in the subject of Yog and Sanatan Kriya bore fruit. It was her faith that caused the miracle. In spite of doctors the world over saying that she would never speak, Abha's daughter now not only speaks but also chants ***mantras****. Actually, a mother's tears can not only move mountains but also can invoke and bring forth the blessings of the Divine forces that run Creation. Yog is the final frontier and its energy is very much achievable even by regular people. Her story is proof:*

Even recounting this story is traumatic for me but let me tell you how I survived the most horrifying phase of my life:

I was on the verge of losing my young daughter to a bizarre accident. It was April 2, 2006. She was on the playfield. Spotting her father outside, she ran towards him. In her excitement she didn't see a steel wire pulled taut along the boundary and ran straight into it. The wire slit her wind pipe or trachea into two halves and nearly cut through her food pipe too.

My husband, a Colonel, posted in Delhi at that time, rushed her to the Indian Army's Research and Referral Hospital (R & R) where she was immediately put on the ventilators in the Intensive Care Unit (ICU). An emergency surgery was carried out. The operation lasted for a grueling seven-and-a-half hours. Even after that, the doctors were unsure about her survival. We were asked to wait and watch for the next 72 hours. It is during this critical time that we were guided to Yogiji by a doctor at R & R who happened to be one of his followers. The doctor didn't

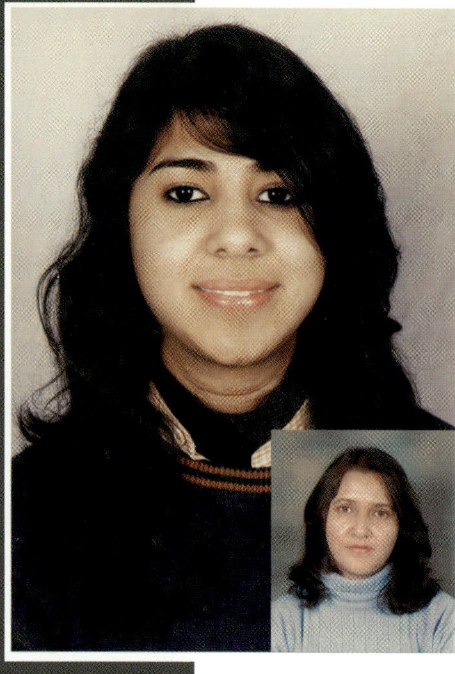

Like daughter, like mother.

give us any false hope about the meeting, just a quiet assurance that Yogiji would be able to tell us as to what to expect.

We met Yogi Ashwini on April 4, which was a great privilege as it happened to be His birthday. Yogiji assured us that our daughter would recover and would be walking after six days. We wanted to believe Yogiji but her deteriorating condition, indicating the opposite, made finding faith difficult. The next day onwards He started healing her spiritually while she was still in the ICU.

My daughter started responding, which was nothing short of a miracle for us. And a greater miracle was that she actually walked on the seventh day, exactly as Yogiji had predicted.

Yogiji is neither a doctor nor a scientist, but at every step He could see and tell what the latest technology and top doctors could not. He starts where medical science stops.

Our ordeal was, however, far from over. Two months later when she was discharged from the hospital, it was with the tragic pronouncement that she would neither be able to breathe normally nor recover her speech. Evidence bore out the doctors' opinion: she had badly damaged nerves, chords and larynx, and she was breathing through a tracheotomy tube attached to her neck.

Yogiji, however, maintained that she would be okay.

We took her to the best doctors in Delhi and Bombay in India and even in the UK and the US. But alas, all of them gave a uniform response, confirming what the R & R doctors had said.

But most doctors believe in challenging their limits. After six months, they recommended a surgery aimed at piercing her paralyzed vocal chords in order to allow a small passage for breath. This would also facilitate a dim voice, they said.

However, Yogiji stood firm against the idea, and told us to hold on.

Having experienced His guidance, we ignored the medical advice which an expert later told us would have disabled her for life. Yogiji eventually guided us to a super specialist in lyrengeo-tracheal surgery, a Swiss doctor, Dr. Munier who was visiting Mumbai at that time. The doctor virtually reconstructed the trachea. The operation was successful but the doctors' verdict about the loss of voice being permanent remained unchanged. As did Yogiji's verdict. My daughter would speak. He just smiled and said, "Wait for 2 years".

After six months, all the instruments were removed. Almost a whole year passed between the time of the accident and the two major surgeries she underwent. And, it was time for my daughter to appear for her Xth Board examination. Battling through her recovery, the last thing on our minds was her exams or what her scores would be. We would have been grateful if she had just passed but even here we were in for a great surprise. She scored 81 percent marks.

Then Yogi Ashwini prescribed some *kriyas* and *mantras* which she practiced regularly. After a month she asked Him where she was heading. His reply, "your whisper is converting into sound," seemed strange to her as well as us because we could hear no sound. When we did hear 'the sound' after a month-and-a-half, we understood that He had heard it much before we could. Despite a string of miracles, we can never stop being amazed. Neither can our friends and family. Today, my daughter's speech is quite audible and it is improving by the day. Throughout the long struggle, I knew it was nothing but Yogiji's grace that was at work. I mention His name helplessly and repeatedly because it is He who has been guiding us at each step. In spite of the doctors' opinion being the opposite at every step, it is He who has said that her recovery would eventually be complete..

Yogiji is neither a doctor nor a scientist, but at every step He could see and tell what the latest technology and top doctors could not. He starts where medical science stops.

As parents, we'll always be indebted to Yogiji for all that He has done for us and our daughter. She wouldn't have survived without His grace and she wouldn't be normal but for His grace. His blessings are always with us. Today she breathes normally, eats normally and speaks normally; like Yogi Ashwini says "Yog is about being normal".

Abha Chopra

44 years, HOMEMAKER

ARMY HOSPITAL RESEARCH AND REFERAL
DELHI CANTT, NEW DELHI - 110010

TO WHOMSOEVER IT MAY CONCERN

This is to certify that Miss Avantika Chopra, daughter of IC-38651A Colonel B Chopra, had met with an accident in Apr 2006, in which she had sustained severe injury to her neck (windpipe and foodpipe), resulting in laryngeo tracheal separation and oesophageal tear. She has undergone major operations for reconstruction of her windpipe and foodpipe, the latest operation being on 17 Feb 2008. She has bi-lateral vocal chord paralysis and is physically challenged due to breathing and voice disorders. She is breathing with the help of a tracheostomy tube and cannot speak due to a stent placed in her trachea.

(संजीव बधवार)
(Sanjiv Badhwar)
सर्जन कप्तान
Surgeon Captain
वरिष्ठ सलाहकार (कान, नाक, गला एवम् सिर व गर्दन कैन्सर)
Senior Advisor (Ent & Head Neck Onco Surgery)

Laryngo tracheal stenosis

Ms. Avantika Chopra
15years female

2-4 -06 Neck trauma with steel wire Laryngo tracheo esophageal injury. Cricotracheal separation, cricoid #, thyroid # and esophageal tear. Emergency repair of the larynx, trachea and TO fistula was done with Tracheostomy. Laryngeal stent kept.

10 -8 06 Subglottic narrowing 6 mm in diameter and 1.5 cms in length.

21-4-06 Stent removed after three weeks

21-3-07 CT scan neck NED

Dr Monnier's Findings & Comments: 26/03/07

→ Dyspnoea on exertion

→ tracheostomy corked during daytime

→ Bilateral vocal cords palsy

→ Check scopy to see for subglottic stenosis; if stenosed then correct it and keep her on tracheostomy so that nerve innervation can be done at a later stage.

On 16/2/08 just before surgery at Prince Aly Khan Hospital Mumbai,
Dr Monnier writes,
"Trade off between voice & airway has been explained and choice given to patient"

Stent was removed by Dr. Sultan Pradhan at Prince Aly Khan Hospital in Mumbai, 2008.
In 2009 Tracheostomy tubes were removed in R & R Hospital in New Delhi, yet Avantika could not speak . Compromised-Voice.

02 the ultimate bargain

GURUSPEAK

*Ambuj, a typical businessman, had come to my **ashram** to gain something, and of course at a cheap cost (I think he knew that at Dhyan Foundation we don't charge anything and **gyan** is imparted as per the **Guru-shishya parampara**). Well, he got what he was looking for of course, what he paid, he would never understand. But still, it was a profitable deal for him, profits which he will enjoy for many lifetimes to come. And the price? Well, that he has already paid and forgotten. Just regular practice and commitment to doing **sewa** gave him the basic saffron aura. The result was that his thoughts began to manifest.*

*But he is a little frivolous and embedded into the physical. He gets easily swayed with physical gains. I suggest that he be cautious and not deviate from the path of **sewa**-whether he stays with me or elsewhere. Doing business with the subtler layers of Creation is definitely not recommended.*

*The saffron aura is not easy to maintain and requires a great deal of regularity, practice and "**eka tattwa dhyan**".*

My stationery business took me into the deep interiors of Delhi's famous bazaar, Chandni Chowk. The congestion and the noise pollution were maddening. The fact that I had to drive down from my house in Janakpuri, at the very other end of Delhi, made it even worse. So, by the end of the day I used to be completely drained.

Coming home was no relief either as my alcoholic father was a major source of tension for the family. It also caused verbal duels between him and my mother. No amount of counseling would help my elderly father.

I hated the idea of my children growing up in such an environment. At the same time, I was anxious to keep the family together and my business going. The constant anxiety began to take its toll and, at 35, I was already suffering from old age problems. My health, emotions and finances being in a state of turmoil, life was anything but pleasant.

A dear friend who had been watching my steady decline suggested that I attend a Sanatan Kriya workshop. I was desperate for help and enrolled as a student.

The first day, we were taken through the *kriya*, and made to sit in *dhyan*; things that were completely alien to me. What followed was amazing. I have no words to describe it but I will do my best...

My body felt light like a feather, it also tingled; my mind soared as if it was on cloud nine and I felt a rare peace envelop me. I felt so safe, like a baby ensconced in a mother's arms. I was spell bound by the experience. What I saw when I opened my eyes is truly beyond words.

I will try and describe it as well as I can: I saw a saffron-clad, curly-haired, tall, well-built, handsome man with big beautiful eyes, smiling; adorned with *rudraksha* garlands around His neck, arms and wrists, and a golden light all around His head. This golden light was blinding. It illuminated the details of this Divine being standing right in front of me. The feeling of being in my mother's arms returned. My whole body became still. I had never experienced anything like this before. I heard a faraway voice telling me that Yogiji, who had formulated Sanatan Kriya, would be visiting the *dhyan* session. I blinked, thinking all that I saw was my imagination; I shifted my legs to feel awake. When I felt fully awake, I saw Yogi Ashwini in front of me. I looked into His eyes; a pointed beam of light emanated from His eyes and entered my eyes. I didn't blink. Then, He talked about many things including the fine points of the *kriya* and I noticed that He laughed very easily. The atmosphere was so relaxed.

By the time the session ended I got a feeling like I belonged here, with the Dhyan Foundation. I felt at home, literally and metaphorically.

Back home that night, my wife asked me to take my daily medication for blood pressure. For a change, I decided to check the pressure before taking the medicine. Little did I expect what I saw! My BP was 79-118, finally normal after years!! I screamed with joy as I shared the news with my wife.

She just smiled, and said, "Yogi Ashwini has performed this miracle for you. You don't need the medicine now", and her words came true, and I have not needed the medicine since then.

Yogiji also blessed me with *sewa* soon after the first meeting. Within weeks, my business expanded and I got busier than ever. But the happy story does not end here. Within two months of me doing the *kriya* my father let go of the bottle! There can be no bigger miracle than this: it was I who was doing the *kriya* but my whole family was benefitting. My mother's joy knew no bounds. Her life-long wish had come true. All thanks to Yogiji. Don't blame me for being a fanatical practitioner of Sanatan Kriya. My life revolves around it.

Ambrij Sharma

39 years, ENTREPRENEUR

SKIN CARE & FAMILY HEALTH CLINIC

✆ : 0161-2410939
RAM PARK, BASANT ROAD, COLLAGE ROAD, CIVIL LINES, LUDHIANA.

Dr. Y.C. MINOCHA
M.D. (A.I.I.M.S)
Consultant Skin & Sexually Transmitted Diseases

Dr. (Mrs.) KAMLESH BALA MINOCHA
M.D. (A.I.I.M.S)
Consultant in Therapeutics & Family Medicine

Amit Jain 37 M

DATE 6/3/09

No active disease. Over. Genital skin.

[signature]

CONSULTATION HOURS

Morning : 10.00 A.M. to 1.00 P.M. Evening : 5.00 P.M. to 7.30 P.M.

CLINIC CLOSED : Sunday Evening & Monday (Full Day)

03 from darkness to light

GURUSPEAK

Amit is a typical Punjabi businessman, brash and calculative to the core. The first time he saw me I could feel his brain whirring. He was wondering whether I could somehow bring all his problems to an end. The question was clear in his head and he wanted the answer. He wanted to do a profitable deal.

He was willing to risk it all. It was like another venture for him. (He had sensed my aura and was more or less certain that it was a reasonably sure project, and that he could trust me.) His faith in Sanatan Kriya was firm. He knew that it had to work or he would be doomed. His call was answered by my Guru almost instantly. Amit's physical self responded immediately. His emotional and financial state took a year to stabilize.

Today he knows that he made the right investment, and that the deal was indeed profitable.

My life was in a mess. With each passing day the feeling that I was good for nothing and that life was a burden was strengthening its grip over me. I don't know what would have happened to me had I not met Yogi Ashwini. One single meeting changed my life--from being in darkness to never-ending happiness and success. What would one term it; a miracle? Well in my case, ever since I have met Yogiji, every single day of my life, I witness a miracle. There are just too many to count. Earlier, I was a complete wreck and had no faith in God. Somehow, a relative convinced me to come to Delhi and meet Yogi Ashwini. Reluctantly, I came for a Dhyan Foundation session on Yog on Sunday. In the very first meeting I knew I was face to face with a true Yogi. I have no words to describe Yogi Ashwini's enigmatic personality. The moment He entered, the whole room glowed with His presence. I was awestruck. During Yogiji's talk I could only see bright white light all around Him, enveloping the entire room. When Yogiji asked us about our experiences I didn't open my mouth thinking that if I narrated all that I had seen, the others would take me to be a nutcase. It was beyond my comprehension. After the session I moved towards Yogi Ashwini. I just stood there watching Him and He smiled at me. It was spell-binding.

After that day it seems that all my sorrows have vanished ...

I was on medication for 13 years for a serious skin problem. It got cured within a week of

The call of Divine?

meeting Yogi Ashwini. I have not fallen sick ever since. (And is this any less than a miracle?) I had a legal problem for which I was fined 4.5 crore rupees (approximately 9 million USD) and an equal penalty for my brother and father. By Yogiji's grace, I have won the legal case and that penalty stands reduced to near nothing. On the business front, I had an export project for motor vehicles (motor-bikes and three-wheelers), which had been hanging for a long time. One day, I just mentioned it to Yogiji who gave me a name for my motorbike. The next thing I know, the project was on!

I have no rational explanation for all this. All I know is that ever since I met Yogiji, there isn't a problem to which He hasn't given me a solution. Be it money or any other requirement of mine, a mere mention of it to Yogiji is all it takes for it to be fulfilled. I had a disturbed childhood that left scars on me. I was unstable and destructive before meeting Yogiji. Now, I am the opposite. My family and friends are incredulous at the change which has also given them a lot of joy.

All I know is that ever since I met Yogiji, there isn't a problem to which He hasn't given me a solution.

I feel at peace and happy all the time. Even in my interactions with people around me, I feel a new and harmonious connectivity. I think I have been born again. And I can't help but repeat the *sloka* which Yogi Ashwini chanted when He first saw me:

"Asato ma Sadgamaya

Tamso ma Jyotirgamaya

Mrityor ma, Amritam gamaya"

36 years, ENTREPRENEUR

Amit Jain

04 rediscovering sikhism

GURUSPEAK

*Creation is a sum total of various kinds of opposing forces, as are we. Lord Ganesha is the deity which is closest to the physical and his **darshan** is a clear indication that your physical pains and imbalances are now going to go away. In other words, every problem at the physical or emotional level is because there is an imbalance somewhere in the world of energy or **prana**, from where our bodies have manifested. The blessings of Lord Ganesha will definitely help one come out of this state to a natural state of bliss and harmony.*

To call for the blessings of Lord Ganesha, charity and service are a definite way. Anyone, who is selflessly engaged in the service of others is always blessed by this deity.

*Anita, who belongs to the Sikh community, was taught the **Bani** since childhood and the tenets of **sewa** were strongly embedded in her. The problem was just that her **pranic** body was so congested that it was not allowing her to access the subtler worlds. I did not do much with her, just cleared her **shushumna nadi** and lo and behold... instantly, she came to a state of balance and her interaction with the subtler worlds was facilitated. She is happy now as not only can she interact with the forces which run this Creation but now she can even interact with her Gurus in subtler states and dimensions, which was her childhood dream.*

I belong to an extremely orthodox and religious Sikh family. So the idea of Yog, Ganesh *Stuti* and Sanatan Kriya were alien to me. But just because my daughter was going to the Dhyan Foundation, I too followed suit.

To tell the truth, it was not because I was interested, but to see what attracts her so much that she is ready to miss her parties and night-outs at this young age. But the very thought of sitting on the floor and that too for an hour or so, meditating, was an absolute no-no for me.

To be frank, I was a complete physical and emotional wreck at the age of 46. Physically, I was a mess and my nervous system had collapsed due to overdose of medicines, which I would take to ward off bouts of depression.

I still remember my first session of *dhyan*. My awareness was confined to my physical discomforts. I could not think of anything other than the fact that my whole body was aching and I wanted to just scream out in pain. But this was my last encounter with pain.

The moment Yogi Ashwini's grace fell on me everything changed. I was completely taken aback the first time I met Yogi Ashwini, or rather saw Him. I kept rubbing my eyes in disbelief but the image of Lord Ganesha would not disappear from where Yogiji was standing, and interacting with everyone. For me to see Lord Ganesha was strange, for I only worshipped Guru Granth Sahib and went to *gurdwaras* religiously. Following any Hindu deity was out of question. After the session, when my daughter introduced me to Yogi Ashwini, He smiled and said "I know you". I felt a gentle and soothing sensation around my chest and felt as if a strong weight had been lifted off my chest. I felt very light and elated at the very first meeting and I was in a complete daze when I left.

Concepts like *chakras* were alien to me. Leave aside seeing them, I wasn't even aware they existed. But now, I've experienced the *mantras* and deities I had not heard of or seen before. From being a roller coaster ride earlier, today, my life has become a boat, sailing smoothly in the ocean of life. It is as if someone has taken complete control over my actions. If anything goes wrong, Yogi Ashwini always has a solution for me. Physically and mentally, I am changing and becoming stronger day by day.

One day I invited some of my friends for a tea party and before I realized, it ended in a proper *dhyan* session. Since then, every Thursday, I have a *dhyan* session at my house with my friends. Being from a Sikh family, there could have been a lot of objections. So I used to keep things hush-hush until I realised I was wrong, for when you are living in the light of Yogi Ashwini's grace, all obstacles are overcome with ease. There's never been any objection, till this very day...

And according to Yogi Ashwini, if you share the knowledge with others, the knowledge or His grace flows through you. Today when I look back, I have long forgotten the physically broken and emotionally distraught Anita of old. Going to Dhyan Foundation has set me free. I have seen a lot of miracles happening to friends around me, but those are their experiences. My new self is my own experience with the grace of Yogi Ashwini and of course, conducting *dhyan* in my house is something which we couldn't have dreamt of!

Anita Kaur

47 years, HOMEMAKER

I kept rubbing my eyes in disbelief but the image of Lord Ganesha would not disappear from where Yogi Ashwini was standing.

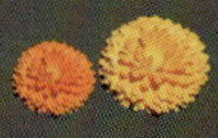

05 the magical healer

GURUSPEAK

Anjana... for her story, I will have to take you to a time when the Moghul empire is in its nascent stages. Raids are a common feature; I am near the outer reaches of Rajasthan. Somewhere around present-day Bikaner, there is a small ***ashram*** *where a* ***sadhika*** *is immersed in deep penance.*

Suddenly the ground shakes under charging hooves; a raid is in progress on the nearby village. She continues to sit with her eyes closed. The scene changes and she is sitting with a group of men and women who look like cow-herds. They are explaining their plight and suddenly someone comes running and speaks in a dialect which I don't understand. There is anger on her face and then it all goes blank. In the next image, I see her on horseback with a sword in her hand and then there is silence.

I can safely infer that her penance was broken and she was forced to pick up the sword to defend her people. Her stage obviously was a very initial stage of ***sadhna*** *where she had to herself pick up the sword. It is said, if one is an evolved* ***sadhak****, then a very significant incident happens in one's life which takes us away from the path and then again in another lifetime, another such incident, perhaps in the form of a misfortune, occurs, which sets us off in search of our Guru and begin our practice once more.... This is typically such a case.*

A debilitating auto immune illness that dragged on for over two years drilled my life with despair, angst and pain. As a bed-bound person, I didn't think I had any blessings to count. But I was wrong. I discovered that on August 15, 2006, I would begin my freedom from torment and torture. It was that day, that I met Yogi Ashwini.

I had experimented with many alternative therapies unsuccessfully and had met most of the so-called Gurus and well-known healers, and come off worse for wear. So, I was circumspect and pessimistic when I went to meet Yogiji. I was sitting in the hall at the Aurobindo Ashram in New Delhi as I was unable to stand. While my friend spoke to a couple of people, I kept to myself. Suddenly, I saw a well-built person stride into the *ashram* and a huge group of people chasing Him for an audience. It was none other than Yogi Ashwini.

Yogiji was giving them a patient hearing when He suddenly started walking towards me. I sprang up from the floor and greeted

Him but was speechless after that. I simply didn't know what to say to Him. He gazed at me and then told me all about my state of health. And everything He said was true to the last alphabet. I was incredulous as I hadn't uttered a word! And neither did anyone there know my state.

For two years I had been telling doctors, therapists and alternate healers about my problem but no one seemed to understand. Modern science, I presumed, could neither figure out nor cure my illness. And here was Yogi Ashwini, who, within nanoseconds of our meeting, told me exactly what I was suffering from!

He directed me to a large hall where people had just finished *dhyan* and were waiting for Yogiji's discourse. As He spoke, I felt each of His words touching me. It was as though He was speaking only to me. I cried silently throughout the discourse and felt a surreal connection with Him. After the discourse, I went to meet Him. He told me that because of the enormity of my problem, it would take me at least a year to start recovering but that eventually my recovery would be complete. That was a great assurance for me. As predicted, the first year was extremely tough. He did not recommend any *kriya* for me, just asked me to be present during *dhyan*.

And here was Yogiji, who within nanoseconds of our meeting, told me exactly what I was suffering from!

After a year though, I could see myself heading towards a normal and healthy life as my fatigue levels, breath and heart rate, which had been frighteningly high, reduced markedly. My sunken eyes began to look a little bright; I could walk a little more than the 200 meters I could hitherto manage; I was certainly more mobile than earlier and could even run small errands. The psychological effect of this physical improvement was remarkable and I became optimistic about my future.

My husband and kids, who had lost all hope about me bouncing back to my lively old self, were thrilled. Today, they are there to testify that I am the person they knew me to be before illness struck. And it is all thanks to Yogi Ashwini.

After spending a little less than two years in Delhi, we had to relocate to Bangalore. That was certainly not something I was looking forward to. But willy-nilly we shifted in the summer of 2008.

Once in Bangalore, a new determination came over me: to share what I had received from Yogi Ashwini with others. So, I began to search for a place to start the Bangalore chapter of Dhyan Foundation. Slowly, a whole lot of people got attracted to the Foundation and today the bustling Bangalore Centre is testimony to the 'power of one.' And that 'one' is none other than Yogi Ashwini.

I will sum up my miraculous recovery and my new life with these words of a Spanish monk: "Sometimes God withdraws a particular blessing from someone so that the person can comprehend Him as something other than just a being of whom one asks favours and makes requests. He knows how far He can test a soul, and never goes beyond that point. At such moments, we must never say, 'God has abandoned me!' He will never do that, even though we may sometimes abandon Him. If the Lord sets us a great test, He always gives us sufficient Grace to pass that test."

I am not just grateful for the bountiful Grace but also for being guided to my Guru who lights my path at each step. He has unraveled my potential to me.

Thanks to Yogi Ashwini, the journey of my spirit is now also a spirited journey.

Anjana Rajguru

36 years, WRITER & JOURNALIST

ANJANA RAJGURU REPORT

Dr. M. Gourie-Devi
MD, DM (Neuro), DSc(Hon), FAMS, FIAN, FNAS
Honorary Advisor for Neurological Research
Indian Council of Medical Research
Emeritus Professor (Neurology)
Institute of Human Behaviour and Allied Sciences (IHBAS)
Formerly, Director/Vice-Chancellor
Professor and Head of Department of Neurology,
National Institute of Mental Health and
Neuroscience, Bangalore
President of Neurological Society of India

Senior Consultant Neurologist
Administrative in Charge
Clinical Neurophysiology Laboratory
Department of Neurology
SIR GANGA RAM HOSPITAL
Rajinder Nagar, New Delhi - 110060, India
Pvt. OPD, Tel. : 25762672-74
EEG/EMG Lab. 25735205-13 Extn. 1042
Address for Correspondence
Resi. : Flat 9, Doctors' Apartments,
Vasundhara Enclave, Delhi - 110096, India
Tel. : 22618573, ~~22617977~~ Mob. : 9811950100
E-mail : gouriedevi@hotmail.com

Mrs. Anjana Rajguru 2/5/2005
34 yrs.

In Sept 2004 had pain in (Rt) interscapular region.
In Oct 2004 – had an episode of severe pain in the back with muscle spasm.
Has multiple symptom – pain in different region of body.
Palpitation → tachycardia.
Itchy feeling.
Excessive tiredness.
All symptoms are aggravated 7 days before + during periods.

Anxious personality.
Fibroadenoma (Lt) breast –
No H/o hypertension & diabetes
Has been treated with antidepressant, NSAID, physiotherapy, laser therapy, diathermy – with variable short lived improvement –
Presently on homeopathic Tr.

O/E. Tender spots – both trapezi L>R.
2nd Costochondral R – L.
Suboccipital R.
Supscapular R.
Paraspinal – R.
Greater trochanter. R.
Ankle L R
Knees – R.

55 Kg.

Dr. S. K. Chadha
MS., Mch, FIACS FNCCP
Senior Consultant
Cardiothoracic & Vascular Surgery

• SIR GANGA RAM HOSPITAL MARG, NEW DELHI - 110060 ☐ ✆25735205 (10 Lines)
Fax : 011 2575-1002 ☐ **E-mail** - gangaram@sgrh.com **Website** : www.sgrh.com
• CLINIC : **Sir Ganga Ram Hospital**, Private OPD 2 PM to 4 PM (Mon to Sat)
Room No. 138, Tel. : 25762672 / 73/74 Extn. 1138, 1176
• **Holy family Hospital** Okhla New Delhi **tel. : 6845900 - 909**
RESIDENCE : X-32, Green Park (Main) New Delhi - 110016 **Tel.** : 26967004, 2651 4821, 2685 4651

21.07.04

MRS - ANJULA GUJRAL
Age 45 YRS

Diag — CVI Rt leg
with Thrombophlebitis.

Inv —
. Venous Doppler Both legs
. Blood Hb TLC DLC ESR

Rx —
0 —— 0 . Tab Ciplox TZ 500mg BD × 1 wk
0 —— 0 . Tab Daflon 500mg BD
0 —— 0 . Tab Rantac 150 BD
— — 0 . Tab Ecosprin 75mg HS
0 — — . Cap Becosule Z 1 OD
. Elastic stockings day dy
. Elevation of legs day night
(} 2 Wks)
. Rev after 2 Wks

[signature]

06 a subtle walk into a new day

GURUSPEAK

When Anjula approached me, she was already on the wrong side of forty. Her body had been weakened, having taken too much strain in her worldly duties of bringing up a family. She never had the time to look after herself, hence this problem which normally happens when your circulatory system [of which the heart is a major part] begins to grow weak. In the etheric world it is called a malfunction in the ***moolchakra*** *and* ***anahat chakra****, because of which the* ***pingala nadi*** *[which is responsible for keeping the blood flow normal] had become incapable of transferring* ***prana*** *from the* ***mooladhar*** *to the* ***anahat****, the result manifested in her legs which are normally the first to get affected because of this imbalance. Simply putting in fresh violet* ***prana*** *in her* ***pingala nadi****, temporarily, had the effect of correcting the imbalance.*

Anjula's dedication to the subject and her practice strengthened the ***pingala*** *on a permanent basis and finally the heart also was rejuvenated. I can say now that she has gotten over the imbalance and I am not expecting her to fall sick now, at least for as long as she remains a practitioner of the Sanatan Kriya.*

Certain things leave such an impression on your mind that even months and years after the event, they remain embedded in you. One such event was when I met Yogi Ashwini; the energy left me spellbound when I met him the very first day and it keeps me mesmerized to this day.

I still remember, it was in the winter of 2003-2004. I started experiencing a terrible pain in my lower right leg. I ignored it till July'04. By then it got worse. A lot of patchy blue marks had appeared, starting at my heels and midway up my right leg. The pain too became unbearable. I was then forced to consult Dr. S.K. Chadha, senior consultant, cardiothoracic and vascular surgery at Sir Gangaram Hospital.

A Doppler test was carried out on both my legs. The images very clearly revealed that the blood flow in my left leg was normal, whereas in comparison, the flow in the right leg was extremely sluggish and weak. The doctor's diagnosis - Blood Insufficiency Syndrome. The valves in the veins of my right leg, which are responsible for transporting the blood upwards to the heart, had considerably weakened. There is no permanent cure for this condition, except that I would have to wear long, thick stockings for the rest of my life or else may even have to undergo a major surgery.

In October'04, I had the good fortune of coming under Yogiji's guidance at Dhyan Foundation. That was the day when I literally

That was the day when I literally experienced what it is to meet an evolved person, and what exactly is a miracle.

experienced what it is to meet an evolved person, and what exactly is a miracle. When I told Yogi Ashwini about my painful problem, He just smiled and I felt a tingle run through my spine. A week later when I met Yogi Ashwini, He asked me about the pain. I was dumbfounded because it was then that I realized that I had not felt any pain or any discomfort ever since I felt that tingle in my spine, the week before. I had experienced a miracle first hand.

Anjula Gujral

50 years, TEXTILE DESIGNER

07 rationalising the world of ether

GURUSPEAK

Anumeet is a typical research scholar. In every lecture of mine her questions would become more and more technical and confusing, for her. She wanted to rationalise just about everything with her logical mind and wanted a logical answer to nearly everything that I spoke about.

The good thing about her was that she was willing to do whatever I told her and that also without a question or doubt. That is just about all that one needs to open the doorways to the inner world and it did open them for her and that also within a few months. On the physical plane some of her pains and aches just disappeared and on the spiritual, she began having ***darshans*** *of Sikh Gurus and the deities which control Creation. I can say that now her logical and physical brains are both satisfied.*

As a research scholar, the long hours of study had taken their toll on my body. I had trouble sleeping and had extremely low immunity levels due to which I was perpetually sick and lethargic. At the age of 22, the muscles in my right hand became so weak that writing and typing became increasingly painful, a problem diagnosed as 'writer's cramp'. Since the nature of my work demanded writing a lot, I resorted to heavy medication which only deteriorated my health further. I came to Dhyan Foundation a few months back and the first thing that Yogiji told me, "stop all medicines at once". He also asked me to do the Sanatan Kriya regularly. The effect was immediate; my insomnia, tension and lethargy just disappeared. I was sleeping well and was more energetic, as well as calmer. On my second meeting He graciously gave an oil for my hand. I applied it barely three times and my right hand became as good as new. It was a miracle straight out of some story book, just like magic. My pains and aches have since vanished. In fact, I have not felt the need to take any medicines at all. Not even a Disprin! I work double the hours I used to and have never experienced such strength and glow before. Being an academic with a scholarly background, these experiences reaffirmed my faith. I experienced a deeper connection with my Sikh roots. The word 'Guru' was always 'revered' in our family and for me it was a four letter word which should be honoured and respected, but, could never understand the power and force which it commanded. My brain knew its power, but my soul was confused due to lack of experience, Yogi Ashwini took me through certain experiences and then its dimension expanded and encompassed my whole existence. Yogiji made me a 'Sikh' in the

truest sense of the word. Seeing the changes in me, my very rational family realized that 'Yoga' was not divorced from rational thinking. The logic behind every act in 'Yoga' became clear to my near and dear ones. The results were so convincing that my relatives started the Sanatan Kriya without losing any more time in long debates. Yogiji led the way for all of us.

Anumeet Kaur

24 years, M PHIL. HISTORY, STUDENT

08 straight from tapovan

GURUSPEAK

*Bhumika, is blessed with certain psychic abilities because of her intense **tap** in her previous life. She was the **shishya** of Sage Nagraj who lived in the higher reaches of the belts of the glacier Gangotri at Tapovan.*

*She served him for nearly 80 years at a stretch without missing any of his routines. When he was leaving his body he blessed her with the blessing of Guru **sewa** and showed her the path to the next dimension, but since in yet another lifetime, she had caused pain to a lot of animals as a hunter, she was told that till 35 years of her present life she would go through pain in nearly all aspects of her life, whether physical or emotional and then she would be delivered. I think the 35 years should now be coming to an end and a new beginning awaits her... life should begin for her from where she had left it in the upper Himalayas.*

I met with accidents three times, and on all three occasions, I was hurt at the same place- left knee, and right shoulder, thrice in three months. The pain was so intense that I could not even stand.

About that time, I heard about a Dhyan Foundation Yoga session happening in Dehradun. I went just like that, but instead of sitting on the ground, I sat on a chair as the pain in my knee was extreme. When Yogi Ashwini entered, He looked at me and said, "At your age you should not be sitting on a chair and doing the *kriya*." I told Him about the accidents and the excruciating pain in my knee and shoulder. Yogiji cursorily looked at the two problem areas. I had a very different and warm sensation in both the affected areas. Then I went back home and realized that there was no pain.

I realized that it was Yogiji who had cured my pain, and I immediately called up Dhyan Foundation members who had come with Yogiji to inform Him and thank Him for His blessings. Yogiji said, "Just ask her to concentrate on the *kriya* and help others around her." I was surprised how someone could be so apparently oblivious to his powers and divinity.

Today, there is no trace of pain or difficulty in my body. I would say that I am really blessed by Lord Shiv. Since I met Yogi Ashwini, I have felt a kind of energy moving around me which helps me follow the right path. I have been in search of someone who would explain to me the unusual experiences I have been having since I was 10 years old. I used to see strange happenings in my dreams, but no one could explain what they were all about.

Yogiji gave all the answers through yoga. My concepts are much clearer now, as to what was happening then. I was made to experience the subtler dimensions which, I used to see in my dreams ... they are dreams no more ... now they are real.

Lots of changes have happened in my life. Sometimes when I talk to somebody I feel that it is not me who is conversing with the other person but Yogiji's energy.

I get indications during *dhyan* or dreams whenever something is going to be manifested. Initially, I used to be amazed, now this kind of 'pre-image' is routine. Yogiji keeps me moving forward in my life, in harmony and energised. Distractions and hurdles don't disturb me anymore. I am truly happy.

Yogi Ashwini says, "Yoga is not just visions. It is beyond visions." And I have the satisfaction of knowing that I am on the right path and Yogiji is there to give me direction. Yogiji has brought this true and pure yogic culture back to our misled society without any alteration and modification, as it was given to us thousands of years ago through the *Guru-shishya parampara.*

Bhumika Malgari

30 years, MARKETING PROFESSIONAL

No looking back...

09 reshaping life

GURUSPEAK

Chandni was a very ordinary, basic material girl, a very talented fashion designer, whose only desire was to look attractive and be in demand. I used the word "was" because the perfect practice of Sanatan Kriya has completely changed her whole persona. I have not looked at her past lives because I know that she has been specifically sent down to aid the cause of Divinity, which is maintaining the balance in Creation. I know that after this life she will go back to where she has come from. It was the compulsion of experience which was necessary for her to awaken her ***antahkarna*** *and realize her purpose... and she got the desired experience.*

I have gone through the worst nightmare of any twenty year old - being plump! I tried everything- gymming till I dropped, diets and dance classes, walking and jogging... But I lost nothing but hope and gained nothing but depression... With every passing day my hope of getting an hour glass figure was fading away. Extreme work-outs and dieting even had adverse effect on my health. I had an unhealthy pallor and a constant feeling of being tired and lethargic due to the various diet plans.

And then I met Yogi Ashwini. He asked me why I look so troubled. "A twenty year old should be full of life and beaming with vitality." I said, 'it's nothing'. I was too embarrassed to admit the real cause of my anxiety. And then the next thing He told me made me blush and my ears started burning. He asked, "Do you really want that waist?" 'How did He know?', was my question. Though now I know the answer. Nothing is hidden from Yogiji.

It was that day and now, and my complete physical form has changed. Yes, I actually achieved the hour glass figure that I was so desperate for, and that too without any rigid diet plans or exercises. People have actually expressed their desire to have a form like mine. They tell me, "... you look like a model! You've grown prettier, and you have a beautiful glow. What did you do?" And it freaks me out. I did not even tell anyone about my desire, leave aside doing anything about it. Yet it happened and I got much more than I would have cared to ask for. How else can you describe it, but a miracle? It is miraculous indeed how your thoughts materialize just by being in the company of an evolved soul...

Chandni Jain

22 years, FASHION DESIGNER

M R CENTRE - GREEN PARK

Dr. Parveen Gulati M.D.

Name: **MS. DARSHANA JAINI**
Date: **08.03.2002**
Ref. by: **DR. RAVI SAUHTA**

MR Imaging of the lumbar spine was performed in sagittal and axial plane using dedicated quadrature TL coil. SE, TSE and FFE sequences were used to obtain T1 and T2 weighted images. Flow compensation techniques were employed to reduce flow artifacts .

The study reveals loss of lumbar lordosis with straightening of the spine. The size, shape, alignment and signal intensity patterns of the vertebrae appear normal except for mild degenerative changes with end plate degeneration at L4,L5 and S1 vertebrae. There is no pre/para vertebral or any epidural collection. There is no evidence of any active infective pathology.

Intervertebral disc at L5-S1 level shows diffuse subligamentous herniation with prominent posterocentral component with annular tear causing mild compression over the thecal sac and bilateral neural canals relatively more on the left.

There is no significant osteophytic or discal compression at any other level.

Intervertebral disc at L5-S1 level shows degeneration as evidenced by the loss of bright signal intensity of nucleus pulposus on saggital T2W images.

There is no primary canal stenosis. The lower dorsal cord, cord termination and conus medullaris appear normal.

OPINION: MRI findings are suggestive of diffuse subligamentous disc herniation at L5S1 level resulting in mild compression with other findings as described. Please correlate clinically.

DR. PARVEEN GULATI **DR. PIYUSH PANDIT**

Organ Imaging Research Centre (I) Pvt. Ltd.

A-23, Green Park, Main Aurobindo Marg *(Next To Free Church)* New Delhi-16

Tel. : 6866134, 6968196, 6859117, 6859118 *ON PANEL* - BHEL, HOLY FAMILY, INDIAN AIRLINES, DESU, ESI

10 a click is all it takes

GURUSPEAK

Darshana, when I had seen her the first time, had more or less given up on life. Though a very pretty woman she looked haggard and completely dejected.

***Tantra** is a very powerful art and with the blessings of the Guru it actually works miracles, but just that one requires the permission of the Guru before channelising it into anybody and obviously it can never be used to harm anybody.*

*That day was lucky for Darshana as I had got permission to try out an aspect of **tantra** on her. That click which she heard was actually the disintegration of the black forces which had been unleashed on her by a close friend in Pune. The Guru's grace once more bore fruit, and after that in the physical world, she has never looked back. And in the spiritual ....she should progress if she maintains the pace of her practices.*

I entered the world of miracles a few years ago...

I was suffering from a chronic lower back condition. Due to the on and off bed rest I had to take, I started developing spondylitis. The constant giddiness gave rise to gastric and upper respiratory problems. You can quite imagine my physical and emotional state; basically I was just not at a happy place!! At 33 years of age, I was feeling old, helpless and quite depressed. It was only my children that kept me going...

This carried on for about two years. During this time I had been on pain killers, physio-therapy, and orthopedic doctors and finally was asked to consider surgery. This, I was not ready to consider.... I had heard that 'Yoga' had a cure for all. A friend of mine recommended a 'Journey of the Spirit' workshop with Dhyan Foundation and thus began my miraculous recovery. I experienced what 'not being in pain' meant after what seemed like ages. My problems started vanishing one after another....

That day, Yogi Ashwini stretched my back and there was an audible 'click' and my back and I have never looked back!! One would think that this is the end of my story, but I would call it only the beginning of my journey towards being a more aware, a more compassionate, a more responsible person, and a step taken towards being a slightly more balanced human being.

Not a day goes by under the protective umbrella that is Yogiji, when I do not say "My God this is a miracle!" On one of the earlier

occasions when I had an audience with Yogi Ashwini, He asked me, "Why don't you become a teacher?" And today, without any formal background in the field of education, I am a teacher in one of the best schools in Delhi, if not one of the best in the country!! All these miracles are tangible and visible on the physical, emotional and financial levels but the miracles I have experienced on the spiritual level cannot be quantified. They are priceless... I owe my own, and my children's life to Yogi Ashwini.

Not a day goes by under the protective umbrella that is Yogiji when I do not say "My God this is a miracle!"

Darshana Jaini

39 years, TEACHER

11 sakshatkar of lord shiva

GURUSPEAK

Deepti is a seeker, and not only from this lifetime but from many previous births. She has done severe penances to achieve her Guru. I need to mention two specific things about her here. First, that in her last birth she was born to a Brahmin family in Gopeshwar, Uttara Khand in India. Her father, a very learned Brahmin, gave her the Guru ***Mantra*** *just before he left his body. She remained unmarried and chanted the* ***mantra*** *till her last breath.*

Just before she left her body Mahadeva's ***doot*** *Veerbhadra appeared to her and told her that in your next birth you will see Lord Shiva in a* ***Shivling*** *while the people who would be with you would just see a* ***Shivling****. That would be the route to your Guru and finally to Lord Shiva.*

The words of Veerbhadra came true. While travelling through Uttarakhand one day with her family, she fell sick and the car had to be stopped. There was a Shiv temple nearby where her family took her. ***Aarti*** *(ritualized prayers for a deity) was in progress and her folks made a video of the* ***Linga*** *and the proceedings. Then after a while they left, and then the miracle happened. When she saw the video, the image of Mahadeva was clearly visible to her in the* ***Linga****. Her journey began and she found me... or I should say I was blessed to have found her.*

I always had a quest for the spiritual sciences and healing, but in today's world there are thousands of peddlers who for their selfish motives are selling their products and fooling people in the name of yoga and healing techniques. I was in search of someone who could make me experience the spiritual world and at the same time I wanted to be sure that I was not being fooled.

Before coming to Dhyan Foundation I did a healing workshop, out of curiosity, and even paid Rs. 2500, for this two day course. But the feeling of uncertainty remained as I was not aware of where I was heading. I turned to other organizations but the present state of Yoga organizations is such that one feels turned off by their very name. But I kept seeking, and it ended when I met Yogi Ashwini...

Life had never been so meaningful and beautiful earlier. All my worries are gone; Yogi Ashwini is there to take care of me and correct me when I am going wrong. I had never experienced this feeling earlier ever before. Your Guru knows you more than you know yourself. He knows you inside out, even one's latent capabilities, of which one might have remained unaware of.

I still remember in one of the sessions somebody asked me a question on Yoga and I was dumbfounded! I thought I didn't know the answer to it. But Yogiji told me, “Think over it for two minutes and then answer.”

I was completely blank as to what I should say, but when I started speaking, I surprisingly answered exactly the way He would have wanted me to. I don't know how it happened but I was really happy....

The day you meet your Guru, miracles start happening from that very moment; they are tangible proofs of the energy you are with and have their own purpose. Having experienced miracles in all spheres, be it financial, emotional, physical and spiritual, I know about their existence. I will share one such experience of mine...

I was completely blank as to what I should say, but when I started speaking, I surprisingly answered exactly the way He would have wanted me to.

One day I was getting ready for work. My office cab arrived and in the hurry to get up, I twisted my ankle. I literally shrieked in pain and sat down. I had apparently sprained it. I was in tears and the injury was so bad that leave aside walking, I could not even move my ankle. However, since I had some important work in office, there was no chance of taking leave. So with great difficulty and with the support of my friends, I went to work. A short while later, my foot had swollen so much that I could not wear my sandals. Even the pain killers failed to work.

In the evening, one of my friends came to my desk and I generally started talking to him about Yogi Ashwini and the miracles people at Dhyan Foundation have experienced. While talking to him, we realized that it was time to leave and I suddenly got up and started walking fast to get my bag from the office desk. I totally forgot that I had a sprained ankle!!

My friend started laughing and said "How could you walk so fast with that pain in your ankle? I hope you were not joking about it!!" That was when I realized that while I was talking to him about Yogiji, my pain had disappeared completely and the swelling which was making it difficult to slip on my footwear till about half an hour back had almost subsided. I smiled and told my friend that this was Yogi Ashwini's blessing that I was trying to explain to him. He himself had experienced the miracle because he had seen the condition of my foot.

This is Divine Grace, for without any medicine or medical treatment and just by talking about Yogi Ashwini's Divine power, the pain and swelling just disappeared. The look of disbelief in his eyes when he saw my normal ankle was as if he had seen a ghost.

Deepti Mahajan

24 years, FINANCIAL ANALYST

12 disease? where?

GURUSPEAK

Deepak is a seeker, but he was lost in the jargon of the business end of today's spiritual world.

He had gone to many so called spiritual organizations and had tried many commercial minded Gurus to quench his thirst for spiritual experiences and answers, but by the time he came to me the situation was so bad that he had completely lost faith in a spiritual person. He was such a skeptic who even mistrusted the Gita, thinking of it as yet another money spinning trick.

I had to change this as he had phenomenal potential. So all I did was revitalise his liver with a dose of fresh ***prana*** *and luckily for him and me the liver responded and what happened next is best read from Deepak's own words.*

When I came to Dhyan Foundation, the last thing that I expected was miracles and cure from a lingering skin problem. I had this skin problem (a sort of dermatitis) on my left palm. It was spreading slowly to the entire hand, leaving an itchy burning sensation in its wake. The skin had gone red and the upper layer was peeling off.

I tried Unani (a Graeco-Arabic healing system) medication which caused some side effects. For this reason I was avoiding allopathic medicines too. I was rather disenchanted with my ailment and my circumstances when I had my first meeting with Yogi Ashwini.

After *dhyan*, I met Yogiji, told Him about my problem and showed Him my palms. After a mere glance, He said "*doctor ko dikhao, phir mujhe batana woh kya bolta hai?"* (Consult a doctor and let me know what he says).

I thought, 'I have come to Yogi Ashwini for a solution and He is asking me to consult a doctor'. I was rather disappointed. The next day I went to a skin specialist and showed him my palms, and to my utter surprise, the skin problem had disappeared!

When I showed my palms to the doctor there was no redness, no burning or itching. My father who was with me was spellbound. There was nothing to show to the doctor!! My palms were absolutely fine.

When I reached back home, my mother enquired about the skin problem, I said, "it has healed". Even she could not believe her ears. I had been suffering from this problem for such a long time that she did not believe me and instead took my left palm in her hands to see for herself.

Seeing that my left palm had healed perfectly, she took my right palm in her hands. This too was normal; then she asked my father about it, who said, *"Pata nahin! Kal tak toh tha ab jaane kahan gaya?"* (Don't know where its gone. It was there yesterday but today there's no trace of it). Next Sunday when I told Yogi Ashwini about it, He just smiled and said, *"aur batao...?"* (Tell me more).

What should I call this - my good luck, Guru's grace or a miracle? I leave it for you to decide.

Deepak Verma

39 years, DEALER IN COMPUTER HARDWARE

13 a logical miracle

GURUSPEAK

Dr. Gujral, a very successful gynaecologist, she had spent a number of years of her practice at the Radha Swami Ashram hospital, where she treated patients free of charge. There itself, for all these years, she had been trying to learn how to meditate.

Someone who has put in so much of labour to help the poor cannot be an ordinary person. The glow of service was apparent in her the very first time when I saw her. I was really surprised when I realized that even after thirty years of selfless service and yoga, experience of the world of the spirit had eluded her.

With her being a doctor, I knew that nothing short of an unexplained medical miracle would suffice to tell her logical mind about the power of Yoga, which till now was limited only to, and by, her intellectual (mind) experience .

So I requested my Guru to do just that and the rest is explained by Dr. Gujral.

I am a gynaecologist by profession. I was always interested in spirituality, though it is not considered a subject for doctors. However my faith in the power of this science was always very strong.

I met Yogi Ashwini at the Vasant Vihar Club in 2004. In spite of the demands on His time, He talked to me alone for over an hour. I requested Him for His blessings and asked Him to restart my *dhyan* practice, as I used to sit for *dhyan* earlier but had to discontinue it, and that was my concern at that time. He blessed me, and ever since my *dhyan* routine has been in place.

Few months ago, I experienced excruciating pain in my left wrist. There was no trace of any injury. As I am a doctor, I applied a crepe bandage to give rest and support to my wrist but to no avail. The pain was constant and at times so intense that I would stay awake through the night. It continued for sometime.

Few days later, the Foundation organised a workshop for spine and back problems. I attended that workshop, where Yogiji asked me how I was doing. I said, I was alright but did not mention to Him about the pain in my wrist, because I thought in my mind that probably I wasn't giving my practices a hundred percent, and the pain must be due to this inadequacy. And I have no right to tell Yogiji about my problems.

I have always been saying to my self 'first make your self worthy of the Guru's grace, then go to Him'. Yogiji smiled and said *"Doctor saab aap toh sach bola karo"*. (Doctor, at least you should be honest.)

I sat for *dhyan* and during that *dhyan* session in the presence of Yogiji, my pain was completely gone. I was moving my wrist as if it was in a perfect condition. I could not believe that Yogi Ashwini had cured me of that pain even without my telling Him about it.

Such is the grace of the Guru. In spite of our failures, He is always ready to bestow His grace upon us. He has His own ways of putting faith in us. He is all mercy, and merciful, it is we who cannot understand His ways. The miraculous way in which my pain disappeared could only be Yogiji's handiwork. No chemical painkiller can have this effect.

As a doctor, the coming and going of this pain was inexplicable. I have no logical or medical reason for its disappearance and neither can I explain how Yogi Ashwini knew that I had such a severe pain in my wrist...

Dr. Gujral

77 yrs,M.B.B.S,D.G.O, OBSTETRICIAN & GYNAECOLOGIST

I could not believe that Yogi Ashwini had cured me of that pain even without my telling Him about it.

A Unit of Kamesh Bhargava Hospital and Research Centre Ltd.
Phase IX, SAS Nagar Mohali
Ph : + 91-172-2211303, 2211308, 2211309, 5097112
5097113, 5063618 Fax : 0172 - 5094124
OPD : 0172 - 5094125, 4658700

TÜV NABCB QMS 010
DIN EN ISO 9001 : 2000

OPD
4657

Date	04/Jul/2009 11:46	Patient No	P0012212
Reg No	OP029112	Age/ Sex	66 Yrs/ M
Patient Name	MR P.N.MENON	Phone	9878166888
S/o	SH.BHASKAR MENON	Mobile	9872264545
Address	#32/AMARAVATI ENCLAVE/ CHANDI MANDIR{PO}/PKL	Department	UROLOGY
		Print Date	04/Jul/2009 11:47
Consultant	PROF. S K SHARMA (REVISIT CHARGES)		

DATE	DIAGNOSIS BPH grade IV
	The pt. has been on – Tab. Dutas-T 1 tab. daily since Dec. 2007 – TRUS/4.7.09 :- Both kidneys are functioning normally – Prostate 145 cm, Mainly median lobe + left lobe. Seminal vesicles are normal; – Bladder capacity 171 cc + PVR – nil. – PSA = 3.94 Free = 0.922 Ratio = 23.40 % Advised to continue the same treatment + follow-up after 4 months. [signature] 4.7.09

14 sanatan way to a healthy life

GURUSPEAK

Dr. Menon is no ordinary person by any standards. I still remember the first day when he came to see me at Taj Hotel, Chandigarh, where I had gone for a press meet. I was sitting in their conference room talking to the local press about Yoga, when this very frail looking senior gentleman walked into the conference room and removed his shoes before he approached our table. I was taken aback by his dedication. He had never seen me and the level of respect which I saw in his eyes was not anything close to the ordinary. I have rarely seen it in some of my students who have been with me for years.

I knew immediately that his deep faith and reverence would get him his desired results and it did.

I had read various articles about Yogi Ashwini in national newspapers and magazines.

These had fired in me an earnest desire to meet Yogiji. I wanted suggestions from Him regarding my grossly enlarged prostate [fourth grade].

I had heard a lot about the Foundation, about how it functions and reaches out to thousands, on the basis of voluntary work done by its members. Even so, a miracle was the last thing I expected.

To add to my good fortune, I learnt from one of the Foundation's volunteers that Yogiji was to be in my city for a session on Yoga. So taking advantage of this opportunity I went to attend this session and had the good luck of meeting Yogi Ashwini.

Yogiji patiently listened to all my problems and told me to get the tests done again after a month and then went on to hear the problems of others like me who were waiting for a chance to talk to Him. At that time I was taking treatment from a reputed hospital in Mohali but with little improvement in my health.

Although my meeting with Yogi Ashwini was brief, it had a tremendous effect on me. Last time, before going to meet my doctor I took PSA and free PSA counts and found them to be surprisingly within limits.

While doing the rectal truss, the expert who was taking the test was stunned as he saw that the size of the prostate had reduced considerably. This was something unexpected, for both the doctors and me. The difference being that this time I knew the

reason for my improved health but not the doctor. I still cannot forget the look of surprise on the doctors face when he saw the report, and his words still ring in my ears, "Is this your report Dr. Menon? I think it is someone else's...".

I have no words to express my deep seated gratitude towards Yogiji for his blessings as today I find myself to be a much stronger person, both physically and mentally.

Dr. Menon

69 Yrs, RETD. PROFESSOR
NITTTR, CHANDIGARH

15 black magic? my guru is stronger!

GURUSPEAK

Gagan, a frail lady who was emotionally and physically in tatters, her condition was so bad that she had nearly given up on life and was actually looking for an exit route. I still remember the helplessness and the hollowness of her eyes, when I saw her for the first time. It was as if they were imploring me to either get her out of all this mess or show her a way out of this life. Her strong will and regular practice of the ***kriya*** *gave her the right* ***karmic*** *balance and emotional strength to sail out of her worldly troubles and pains.*

Regarding the trouble from the world of the occult, I just need to very briefly say that people who use their knowledge of the occult to harm others are taking a very big risk, and are actually opening the doorways to the nether worlds where the dark energy and evil resides. Opening the doorway not for others but for themselves, and let me tell you with a firm conviction, which is based on my long years of experience studying the world of energy and dimensions that interactions with these dark forces ultimately forces one to leave the world and remain in these hells...........for a long time to come.

I came to Dhyan Foundation five years back. At that time I had a severe physical ailment, a valve in my heart was not working properly; I was under Dr. Kaler's treatment, at Escorts. I was lethargic and weak. Tests were being done and my doctor suggested remedial surgery. I told Yogiji and he said, "Everything will be fine, start practicing the Sanatan Kriya and wait for three months." Next day I was supposed to go back to Escorts to collect my reports but Yogiji's words were so powerful and reassuring that I never went back to the hospital at all. In fact from the day I met Yogi Ashwini, I felt a complete change in my health. I immediately started feeling energetic, light and full of strength. I practiced Sanatan Kriya and within three months all my problems were gone! A sudden change that even doctors could not explain. I have not visited any doctor since. It is while writing this experience that I realized that I had not even collected my reports, because I never felt the need to do so.

The health problem that I was cured of was not in my mind, it was very much there. Reputed hospitals' able doctors knew this. How this problem just disappeared, is something which neither my family doctors nor I can tell. It just disappeared. Actually I know I am sounding strange, but it is true as I have experienced it. Simply put, it is nothing short of a miracle.

As Yogi Ashwini says, "Yoga is a true science of the being's evolution and physical is just the beginning". At that time I was weak and emotionally congested. Today I am a changed person. I am confident, happy and my skin glows with vitality and health. Everyone around me has noticed the difference.

I had been with Yogiji for a couple of years and one day I met with an accident. I hurt myself badly. I started encountering strange incidents and even stranger accidents. Uncanny happenings like finding blood splashed all over my car left me scared and confused. These mis-happenings became a regular phenomenon. I would frequently find bones or *sindoor* wrapped in black cloth and have dreams of spirits and ghosts. I used to feel really scared, and had a strange feeling all the time, as if I was surrounded with black energies from another world. All this used to depress me. I told Yogi Ashwini about these bizarre happenings. He replied, "Somebody has tried some black magic on you." He reassured me and said, "Nothing can harm you, just keep an eye on people around you. Whosoever has done it will be affected immediately." Within a few days I came to know that someone in the immediate family was badly hurt in an accident.

"I am there. Don't worry, *tere ko kuch nahi ho sakta*".

To my horror I came to know that he was a follower of a *tantrik*, who used to do black magic. The *tantrik* did black magic on me prompted by this person. In the next few days, the *tantrik* too was hospitalized with boils all over his body. He died soon after.

I told Yogiji and He said, "I am there don't worry, *tere ko kuch nahi ho sakta*" (nothing can harm you). Reassured, I asked Him what He had done. Yogiji simply said, "Nothing". I know for certain Yogi Ashwini does not believe in violence or hurting even an enemy. He later explained that those who do evil against the will of the Divine get this result because of the law of *karma*.

Even today when I think of that time, tears roll down my eyes. I don't know how to thank Yogiji for getting us out of that darkness unharmed and shining.

Yogi Ashwini says, "When you hold the hand of your Guru with complete faith, the things that can cause physical and emotional problems just disappear." Of course the bottom line is that we have to do as we have been told, in totality and have total faith in our Guru.

Yogi Ashwini not only solved a major health problem of mine but also protected and sheltered me from the evil deeds of our so called family members. Being with Him, has given me the security and assurance that I have never experienced in my life ever before.

Gagan Sidhu

34 years. HOMEMAKER

16 asato maa sadgamaya

GURUSPEAK

Gurdev, a typical ***sardarni****, is strong headed, analytical and her logical mind wants tangible proof for everything. She has fixed thoughts, is highly emotional and highly committed; the latter is most important here.*

I don't remember her saying 'no' to anything. Be it participating in a food distribution event or even giving a lecture to a 200 strong audience on a topic, which I have just given her. The Guru's force does not flow in her; she flows in the Guru's force. Belonging to a Sikh household, it was not difficult for me to explain to her the concept of the Guru. She connected easily and understood the world of the ether. It is the key to yoga, the concept of the Guru, which is the ultimate force, which she imbibed in a short while and immediately began sharing what she had got. This was the key to her physical and spiritual growth in just a span of one year.

I don't see her looking back now. She already has acquired the basic ***siddhis*** *that yoga promises and she applies them for the general good, which yoga prescribes. If she falls sick or gets harmed in any way now, then I would be really surprised... and I have stopped being surprised many years back.*

I joined Dhyan Foundation in July, 2007. What drew me to the Foundation? Well, I saw a positive change in one of my long time school friends who had been associated with the Foundation for about 4-5 months. Positive change? Well, let's put it this way that she was a very outgoing, irresponsible teenager, impulsive and like any average 19 year old, her life just revolved around herself, but this attitude changed 180 degrees. She began to take responsibility for other people besides herself. She had transformed into a sensible, level-headed and thoughtful person. And her commitment towards the charitable activities of the Foundation set an example for all of us.

My expectations from the Foundation were limited as I did not know what I was getting into. My first meeting with Yogi Ashwini was enough for me to decide that this is the place I want to be in and this is the organization I would want to be associated with. If I were to go back and think as to why, I became so serious about *dhyan*... I don't think I'll ever get an answer. It was as if there was some magnetism about Him and with every interaction with Him, I seemed to be becoming a magnet myself. Being an orthodox *sardarni*, I had numerous inhibitions and doubts before attending a *dhyan* session. I was pleasantly surprised when I was not asked to focus on any specific god or deity. After *dhyan*, Yogiji entered the room. To my complete disbelief, I witnessed images of certain deities in particular *mudras* all around Him. The post-*dhyan* 'question-answer' session left me dumbfounded when I heard a German lady describe in detail the form of Guru Nanak *devji*, whom she encountered during *dhyan*. I truly believe now that yoga does not restrict the practitioner from following any definite religion and what one follows is personal discretion. And as Yogi Ashwini says, "In Yoga there is no ritual, lifestyle or diet. Yoga sets you free."

My family has traditionally been following a 'Guruji' for many years and it was expected of us to follow their footsteps, which is why my family initially opposed my decision to go to Dhyan Foundation. My mother hesitantly came to meet Yogi Ashwini to see why her daughter had taken such an adamant stance. After meeting Yogiji only once, she herself joined Dhyan Foundation! What's more, every week a *dhyan* session is held at our house too. This was just the beginning of the miracles which were soon to become a regular part of my life since I joined the Foundation.

It was as if there was some magnetism about Him and with every interaction with Him, I seemed to be becoming a magnet myself.

Physical: When I joined, I was a plump 19 year old; I was a state level basketball player; I had been going to the gym daily since 9th grade, and yet I was overweight. I was active, and had healthy eating habits. So where was the problem? I found that I had a thyroid problem. I got tired very easily, and my nervous system became weak and my body began to shiver. Excessive hair loss, panic attacks and emotional outbursts were common and all this when I was in 12th grade. As if the pressure of board exams wasn't enough, I had to deal with these symptoms. Exactly how acute was my case? Well, the Ref. range of TSH (thyroid stimulating hormone) should ideally be between 0.700 - 5.700 uIU/mL and my test report read a staggering 185! No, I haven't forgotten to put the decimal point. The doctor recommended a medicine but cautioned me that missing my dose would mean that I would go back to square one.

Missing one dose? You won't believe me if I say that the day I met Yogi Ashwini was in fact the last day when I took the medicine. I didn't even realise when I had stopped taking that medicine. After two weeks of meeting Yogi Ashwini, He casually asked me whether I had got my thyroid checked lately. I replied that I did not feel the need as ever since I had met Him I felt absolutely ok.. On Yogiji's advice I got my thyroid checked. When my report came I was completely dumbfounded -- my result was absolutely normal. Medical science may not have an answer to this about turn but I know that it was Yogiji's words and his magnanimous aura that made this 'miracle' happen. Surprisingly I lost those extra kilos without any conscious effort. People comment that I look much more radiant and fitter than ever with each passing day. I just smile and credit it all to Yogiji who made me rediscover myself.

Academics:I was an average student and in my first and second year in college, I managed to score 53% and 47% respectively. I met Yogiji in the middle of my third year and believe me when I say that I enjoyed myself to the hilt and studied sporadically. With minimal preparation, and last minute studying, I took my exams. I was scared of the result. When I told Yogi Ashwini about this He smiled and said, “What you have done is good enough and don't worry, you will get questions from that only.” When the result was announced, I was overjoyed as instead of having to repeat the class I had scored 54%. I am not trying to tempt students to stop studying and solely depend on last minute preparations. The point I'm trying to make is that if Yogiji says something, it has to materialize and manifest in the physical. This is something which I have been practically experiencing since the day I have met Him and I invite you to try it out for yourself.

Emotional: I was a complete emotional wreck, always finding new excuses to cry. Trivial matters triggered emotional outbursts. I felt angry and depressed and was a pessimist by nature. According to me, losing my father at the age of five was the greatest grief a child could ever suffer. I had grown up seeing my mom cry herself to sleep everyday for over two years before she remarried. I should have forgotten the loss because firstly, I was too young to remember anything much and secondly, my step-dad never made me feel that he was not my biological father. He loves me very much. Yet I was crying constantly. Somewhere I must have been unhappy or dissatisfied or fearful or scared or simply sick. But that too is history. One miracle after the other, visions and images of divine beings, constant bliss, happiness at home, more conscious of another's pain rather than my own, all this because of one Divine being. Maybe for you these are just words, but for me it is the truth. I found Yogi Ashwini; is there anything else that I need to run after?

Gurdev Kaur

22 years, STUDENT

Dr Lal PathLabs Pvt Ltd

DIAGNOSTIC CENTRE: 8, WEST AVENUE ROAD, PUNJABI BAGH, NEW DELHI-110 026
PHONES : 4246 3351/52/53/54 FAX :+ 91-11-2522 4866
MAIN LABORATORY: 'ESKAY HOUSE', 54 HANUMAN ROAD, NEW DELHI-110 001

06 4591990
LPL-PUNJABI BGH

DR. ARVIND LAL
M.B.B.S., D.C.P.
Chief of Laboratory Medicine
FMR HONORARY PHYSICIAN TO THE PRESIDENT OF INDIA

DR. VANDANA LAL
M.B.B.S., M.D. (Path)
Chief of Pathology
SHIROMANI AWARD WINNER

Name : MS. GURDEV
Lab. No : 06 4591990
Age : 18 years Sex: F
Ref. By : DR. SUNEET KHANNA

Reg. Date : 07/07/06
Collection Date : 07/07/06
Print Date : 07/07/06
A/c Status : P P

Test Name	Result	Units	Ref. Range
Glucose Fasting & Post Prandial			
Glucose (F)	87.00	mg/dL	(70.00 - 110.00)
Glucose (PP)	91.00	mg/dL	(70.00 - 140.00)
Thyroid Stimulating Hormone (TSH) @ (Ultrasensitive)	**185.916**	uIU/mL	(0.700 - 5.700

Comments:
Thyroid stimulating hormone (TSH) is a glycoprotein hormone produced in anterior pituatory situated in brain. Its function is biosynthesis, storage & release of thyroid hormone and also determination of thyroid gland size. The ability to quantitate circulating levels of TSH is important in evaluating Thyroid function.
Under normal conditions i.e. Euthyroid state levels are 0.35 - 5.50 mIU/L. If thyroid hormone are low , TSH levels rises whereas in high levels of thyroid hormone the TSH levels fall below the normal limit. This is the best screening test for thyroid function.

Increased levels of TSH are seen in cases of Primary Hypothyroidism, TSH dependent Hyperthyroidism, Sub-clinical Hypothyroidism, Thyroid hormone resistance, Hashimoto's Thyroiditis, Non-thyroidal illness (Recovery phase), TSH antibodies, Drugs-Amphetamines, Amiodarone, Ipodate, Dopamine antagonists.

RECHECKED

Test Name	Result	Units	Ref. Range
Insulin, PP @	5.10	uU/mL	(5.00 - 79.00)
Haemoglobin	**11.40**	g/dL	(11.50 - 15.30)

Page 1

Skochhar
DR. SEEMA KOCHHAR
M.B.B.S., M.D. (Path)
Chief of Laboratory

@ TEST PERFORMED AT MAIN LABORATORIES, NEW DELHI

17 its easy to build an empire

GURUSPEAK

Gurjeet ji is a very able businessman, a very practical person with dormant traits of a saint. It is the phenomenal storehouse of ***prana*** *that lies in him, which was a great attraction for me. I still remember the first time when he came to see me. I used to wear a track suit most of the time and had very short hair. I still remember the look in his eyes when he saw me. He looked at me from top to bottom, smiled and left. I also smiled as I saw him turn for I knew that he had actually turned into the dimension of the spiritual world and his experiences of the psychic world shall now begin. And begin they did, and for him in a language which he understood... the language of the physical world. I am sure he realises now that his smile, when he looks at me, is very different from that of the first day, while mine is still the same.*

Our company is a multinational firm, dealing with infrastructure development. From a small construction concern, we've grown to a Rs. 500 crore (1,00,000,000$) company. At that time I had just about met Yogi Ashwini and he asked me about my company. I told him it is about Rs. 50 crore. He smiled and said, "It will go international soon". I was pleased, but did not know how the jump would happen. Later that year I got an opportunity to go to Kabul for a new business tie up. I waited for an appointment with the deciding authority for two days, but on the third day my patience gave way. The fourth day I decided to pack up and come back, but just then Yogiji's words came back to me. I decided to call Him. He just said, "Wait till evening". And sure enough, the contract to build roads in Afghanistan was signed that evening. By the end of the year we were a Rs. 500 crore international company.

A few years ago, we ran into serious problems with one of our international contracts. One of our employers was not happy, and we were very tense about losing the business and harming our reputation. I was so anxious, that I spoke to Yogiji about this. Yogiji said, "Don't worry, he will come around himself" and he did. This was a 'miracle', as the circumstances were not in our favour. Yet, Yogiji's blessings pulled us through.

During routine tests, it was seen that my blood sugar was high. I was admitted to hospital for further investigation. Yogiji said, "Gurjeet ji, you have no problem". And till date my blood sugar has remained under control. These are simple physical experiences that show the love and protection that is Yogi Ashwini. I am glued to the path of *sadhna* because of the internal, deep spiritual experiences that Yogiji has bestowed upon me.

60 yrs, CHAIRMAN, C & C CONSTRUCTIONS LTD.

Gurjeet Johar

18 the shield of the guru

GURUSPEAK

Jaideep was a regular teenager who wanted to live life in the fast lane. He came to me at a time when he was growing up and was going through changes in his emotional and physical body. When you want to achieve something then you are all the time hyperactive. That was his state. His father who is a successful businessman has lots of enemies in the corporate world, inside his organisation and outside. Two such specific people had been trying to harm his son with the help of black magic practitioners. Black magic is real it is not in the mind, it is very much alive and here. It is a very powerful tool for the corrupt and the wicked and can cause harm to those who do not have a Guru.

I have travelled far and wide studying various aspects of the world of the ether of which these black forces are a part, and so, I understand how disastrous these can be if not blocked correctly and on time.

Now, both these people who tried this on Jaideep are very sick physically and mentally and are regularly visiting the doctor. In spite of being financially well off, they are not able to enjoy the blessings of the Divine. I remember Christ's teachings here which say "Do not do to others what you do not want others to do unto you".

I was like a normal teenager; rash, fun loving and absolutely carefree. Partying was my life and I used to love going for car races with my friends. At that time in my life, I met Yogi Ashwini.

Yogiji never stopped me from anything, but one day when I was leaving his office he said suddenly, "Be careful, and don't drive too fast". I laughed off Yogiji's comment and went out.

As usual I was talking on the phone and laughing, driving at a speed of 150 kmph in the city. Suddenly I lost control of the car and it turned in the air thrice. After sometime all I remember was a huge crowd of people surrounding my car and peeping inside to see if I was alive or not. They pulled me out of the car and looked at me as if they were looking at a ghost. In fact I came out unscathed and when I turned to look at my car it was a mass of mangled metal. The car was completely crushed from the sides due to the force of the accident. People couldn't believe how I survived such a major accident.

At that moment, I suddenly remembered Yogi Ashwini's warning. If only I had listened to Him... I also knew that I was safe only

If only I had listened to Him... I also knew that I was safe only because of His grace.

because of His grace.

I called Him immediately and He said, "Don't worry, nothing could have touched you. But just get your right shoulder X-rayed; I think you have an injury there". This time I followed his advice and my family took me to Dr. Amarjeet Janeja, Healing Touch Hospital, New Delhi. The doctor did a general examination and said that it's not a fracture, just a bump on the shoulder which is hurting. But my family had complete faith in Yogiji and insisted that the X-ray be taken.

Yogi Ashwini was right. I did have a hairline injury in the shoulder. The doctor was totally taken aback. That incident made me realise the powers of this Divine personality.

Jaideep Johar

26 years, PROJECT HEAD, C & C CONST. LTD.

19 an honest appeal

GURUSPEAK

Jyotika is a very nice and honest person. With no tricks up her sleeve and no cunningness about her, came to me as she was unwell, scared and confused. If one is a normal human being and honest and true within and without, then the Divine feels the need to send one a Guru and the physical indication is always given to the seeker as a stroke of good luck or an ailment being healed, instantaneously, just like that. This statement she has made about the puzzled look on the doctor's face, is something I hear all the time from exceptional people. Yet again one needs to reiterate that medical science is not redundant but the Divine Order is final.

I used to be a person who would get tense about the smallest of things, constantly anxious and worried. But an amazing transformation took place when Yogi Ashwini took me under His wing. My usual feelings of anxiety and unease disappeared. Initially, I could not understand why I felt light and carefree, but one day during a talk by Yogiji it just dawned upon me, that I was a different person, and a far happier person now.

Before meeting Yogi Ashwini I had gotten my thyroid checked on the advice of a doctor and some problems showed up in my reports. I had not started any medication yet and an opportunity to meet Yogiji came up. I told Him about my problem. He looked at me and said, "Forget it! And don't take any medicine".

This was my first meeting with Him. I came away both elated and confused. But I decided that I would take Yogiji's advice and I continued my normal life without medicines. Some days later, on the doctor's insistence I checked my thyroid again and it was balanced... neither a point up nor down, just totally balanced. I experienced this 'miracle' first hand and only I know the joy I felt when my doctor said, "No need for thyroid medicines."

I remember the puzzled look on my doctor's face. My friends often say, "You are glowing... how come?" I just smile and answer, "Just come to Dhyan Foundation."

When I first met Yogi Ashwini, I was unemployed. Just a short while after my meeting with Him, I got an offer from this company and my deepest desire of being the most important person in the company was fulfilled. I work in Emaar MGF Ltd. and my profile is related to fund management in the treasury department. No money related decisions in the company are taken without my approval.

Dr Lal PathLabs Pvt Ltd

DIAGNOSTIC CENTRE: 8, WEST AVENUE ROAD, PUNJABI BAGH, NEW DELHI-110 026
PHONES : 4246 3351/52/53/54 FAX : + 91-11-2522 4866
MAIN LABORATORY: 'ESKAY HOUSE', 54 HANUMAN ROAD, NEW DELHI-110 001

07 6701043
PP-PUNJABI BAGH

DR. ARVIND LAL
M.B.B.S., D.C.P.
Chief of Laboratory Medicine
FMR HONORARY PHYSICIAN TO THE PRESIDENT OF INDIA

DR. VANDANA LAL
M.B.B.S., M.D. (Path)
Chief of Pathology
SHIROMANI AWARD WINNER

Name : MS JYOTIKA SETHI
Lab. No : 07 6701043
Age : 21 years Sex: F
Ref. By : UPKAAR NURSING HOME

Reg. Date : 12/11/07
Collection Date : 12/11/07
Print Date : 12/11/07
Account Status : NP

Test Name	Result	Units	Ref. Range
THYROID PROFILE, FREE @			
T3, FREE	3.16	pg/mL	(2.30 - 4.20)
T4, FREE	1.03	ng/dL	(0.89 - 1.76)
TSH, ULTRASENSITIVE	6.770	uIU/mL	(0.350 - 5.500)

Interpretation:

TEST	Reference Group	Age	Reference Range
T3, Free	Adults	> 18 years	2.30 - 4.20
	Children	1 - 9 years 10 - 13 years 14 - 18 years	3.37 - 5.06 3.35 - 4.80 2.87 - 4.55

Dr Lal PathLabs

8, West Avenue Road, Punjabi Bagh (W), New Delhi-110026
Tel: 011 - 3040-3250, Fax: 011 - 2522-4866
Main Lab: "Eskay House", 54, Hanuman Road, New Delhi-110001
Customer Service: 011 - 4423-1234, Web: www.lalpathlabs.com

Dr. Arvind Lal
M.B.B.S., D.C.P.
Padma Shri
FMR HONORARY PHYSICIAN TO THE PRESIDENT OF INDIA

NABL ACCREDITED
M 0112

Dr. Vandana Lal
M.B.B.S., M.D (PATH)
Chief of Pathology
SHIROMANI AWARD WINNER

Name : MS. JYOTIKA
Lab. No : 09 3626858
Account Status : C
Report At : 807-UPKAR NURSING HOME

Age : 23 years Sex: F
Referred by: .
Registered : 05/10/09
Printed : 05/10/09

Test Name	Result	Units	Ref. Range
TSH, ULTRASENSITIVE (CLIA) @	5.130	uIU/mL	(0.350 - 5.500)

Interpretation:

Reference Group	Age	Reference Range in uIU/mL
Children	1 - 2 days 3 days - 4 days 15 days - 5 months 5 months - 20 years	3.200 - 34.600 0.700 - 15.400 1.700 - 9.100 0.700 - 6.400
Adults	> 20 years	0.350 - 5.500
Pregnancy	1st Trimester 2nd Trimester 3rd Trimester	0.300 - 4.500 0.500 - 4.600 0.800 - 5.200

One day I had so much work that I missed a transaction meeting with a client. But thanks to Yogi Ashwini's protection, I learnt from my mistake, and even kept my job without losing face in my office. That day I was walking on egg shells till the matter was resolved. My soul sought Yogiji's forgiveness for the blunder I had made in office. And Yogi Ashwini kept me safe.

My work involves a lot of pressure. The decisions taken are dependent on the funds available. Each day brings a different kind of obstacle. One day, while making various fund statements for discussion with the bosses, I made some errors in the cash flow statement of the company and the numbers were not matching. I was going over the numbers repeatedly and was terrified. My heart was racing as my boss was constantly enquiring about the same; all my efforts and my reputation were at stake. How could I present an incorrect statement to my boss? Yet I just could not spot the mistake.

Just then Yogi Ashwini's words, "A Guru carries you on His shoulders and watches you every second," ran through my mind. I just connected with Yogiji from my *anahat,* closed my eyes and just recited, "Yogiji please resolve this problem." Soon I copied the statement on to another sheet and the numbers matched!

My experiences are engraved on my soul, and only I know how tricky the situation was with my health and on the office front. Yogi Ashwini has shown me that he cares at all places, at all times. Miracles are now a way of life for me, or to put it in other words, a Guru is the biggest miracle of this Creation.

Jyotika Sethi

My soul sought Yogiji's forgiveness for the blunder I had made in office. And Yogi Ashwini kept me safe.

23 years, MANAGER, EMAAR MGF LTD.

20 shakti- a double edged sword

GURUSPEAK

*A woman is an embodiment of **shakti**; she was worshipped and kept on a pedestal by the **Vedic** masters. They knew that Creation emerges from the mothers womb [**hiranyagarbha**] and would go back into it for a rebirth. This absolute power of Creation and dissolution rests in every woman. In some it lies a little more and in some a little less. It's just that those without a Guru do not realise this storehouse of energy in them and mostly waste their lives in frivolous actions and pursuits.*

The five senses are directly dependent on this energy. Those who have more, without a Guru's grace, pursue the senses with more vigour and variations and in the end destroy their own bodies, and also the bodies of their near and dear ones. In history we have examples of many such women. To name a few, Madhubala, Marylyn Monroe, Rani Padmini. Those who have the grace give a direction to this force and channelise it for their evolution and in the process become revered [Anusuyia, Jijabai, Draupadi..]. Those who are full of themselves and do not have a Gurus grace, self destruct. Their strong senses do not permit them to accept a Guru. They forget that old age would catch up and no amount of surgical procedures and therapies can undo the bidding of the 'Divine laws'. They leave the world in chaos and are dissatisfied. An interesting thing which I notice here is that a majority of such women are very pretty to look at.

Lata is an example of such a woman. The first time I saw her I knew immediately here's another one. If she can be brought on 'the path' then she can do wonders. If not, then she will destroy herself and her family. Unfortunately by the time she came to me, she'd already had a few organs removed, for which now nothing could be done. However, I tried to give it direction. She now on her own has started Dhyan Foundation centres; her husband who was always in a financial mess, now has a stable job; her children are healthy and she is a very sought after person with a long list of her own followers. The control that she has over her senses is proved by the fact that recently she refused a political position just because her husband asked her to. She is with me at least 50% and this is the result. If this percentage were to go up then there would be nothing in God's Creation which would be beyond her reach.

What I did was actually nothing, I just requested my Guru to channelise this force into a positive direction and that was it.

For me yog is Guru. Guru is yog. He turned my life around 180 degrees (physical, financial, emotional and spiritual). All my experiences happened due to my Guru Yogi Ashwini. Without Him, I may have vegetated. Before I met Him, I was a frequent visitor to the doctor. Medicines and tests were my weekly routine.

I met Yogi Ashwini on the first *Navratra* of 2005. His aura was so strong and peaceful, that I felt as if I had reached my destination. He looked at me and said, "Your body has a lot of power in it, but the condition it is in is because you have not met your Guru." I was stunned as nobody had told Him anything about me, but He knew instantly. My uterus, ovary, appendix and gall bladder had been removed surgically before I met Him. Towards the end of this first meeting He said to me, "Get your eyes tested, you may not need glasses."

But every time my physical condition made me cry in pain, deep inside me I would feel that one day I would meet someone in my life who would elevate my body and soul.

The power of my right eye was 2.50. The next morning I went to get my eyes tested, it was nearly normal. I used to wear spectacles. Yogiji got them removed instantly with just one look. I do not use any spectacles now. This miracle stunned me; I was delighted and relieved that I was at the 'right place'

I used to have frequent, acute headaches which were so stubborn that pain killers could not 'kill' the pain. I used to get vertigo attacks. I had cervical spondylitis. My left shoulder used to be in pain most of the time. After I joined in 2005, within two months all these problems vanished. I have no logical explanation for this. Yogi Ashwini did not prescribe any *asana*, or any posture, other than just doing the Sanatan Kriya and attending the weekly sessions. And yet, the tiresome headaches just left my body. No vertigo, no spondylitis, no pain. There was a spring in my step. Throat and stomach infections were common place for me before October 2005, but now no more. They also disappeared as I continued my *kriya*. I used to have lower back pain due to some injury and my lower spinal curvature had straightened. Earlier, I could not sit or stand for a long time. Even if I stood or walked for some time it would start to hurt but now as I write this testimonial, this problem has totally disappeared. My body had multiple problems and my knee and foot pain which used to surface once in a while never troubled me again. But as I reviewed my old situation with the present I realized that each and every part of my body is a 'miracle' the way it has been cured by Yogi Ashwini. Five years ago I never thought that I would lead a pain-free life, but today all these wonderful things have happened. I don't know in which life I did good deeds that I got a Guru in this life. Before coming to the Foundation, I had never met anyone like Him nor had I searched for Him. But every time my physical condition made me cry in pain, deep inside me I would feel that one day I would meet someone in my life who would elevate my body and soul.

Gently, Yogi Ashwini removed the difficulties in my physical realm and helped me lead a normal energetic life. Yogi Ashwini has removed all my worries, permanently.

Latha Devi

42 years, NATUROPATH, HOMEMAKER

COLONEL DUGAL MEMORIAL DIAGNOTIC CENTRE : ULTRASOUND REPORT

Dr. VARUN DUGAL MBBS, M.D. (MCI-1732)
Consultant in Radio-Diagnosis & Imaging Sciences

DR. ANUPAM BHALLA
MBBS, DNB

- Whole body Color doppler, 3D, 4D, etc.
- Sector, Convex Sector, Linear, Transvaginal, Transrectal

Mrs. R. LATHA DEVI 39/F
REF. BY : DR. POONAM GULATI

08 July 2006
CCN : 2006 - 3891

P2—FTND—LCB 11yrs
Ut. & one ovary –removed
Gall bladder –removed
C/o pain lower abdomen/ pain during defecation—2-3months

FUC of endometriosis

PELVIC U/S
(Using transabdominal & transvaginal probes with color flow)

Vault of vagina is normal—8.4mms in thickness(Normal < 20mm)
Uterus and one ovary are absent(removed)

The visualized ovary is seen, right of midline. Size of right ovary 35x20x20mms(7.0cc) with 14 follicles, measuring 4 to 12mms each with stromal hyperplasia.

A well defined hypoechoic lesion is seen within wall of the rectum. It buldges from its serosal surface and appears contiguous to the right ovary. No intralesional color flow is seen—Rectal endometrioma.

No other pelvic mass lesion is seen.
No fluid is seen in pouch of douglas.

Endometrioma
(R) ovary
Rectum

UPPER ABDOMEN WAS SCREENED:

Gall bladder is absent (removed).

Common bile duct measures 3.0mms in calibre. It is visualized upto terminal end No calculus is seen within its lumen.

Liver, pancreas & spleen are normal.

Both kidneys are normal in size and echotexture with good cortico medullary differentiation, smooth margins, no dilatation of central pelvi calyceal system, no calculus or calcification. Length of right kidney 99mms. Length of left kidney 99mms.

Urinary bladder is normal in outline with no filling defect. Volume of urine before micturition was 165ml & no post micturition residue.

Urinary bladder is normal in outline with no filling defect.

2 files PTO →

Clinic (Ultrasound & Color Doppler) :
C-27, Green Park Extn.
N. Delhi-110016
Tel. : 26967125, 26865531, 26867508

(Closed on Sunday - Saturday Halfday)

TIME :
Morning : 9 a.m. to 1 p.m. (Mon. to Sat.)
Evening : 4 p.m. to 6 p.m. (Mon. to Friday)

12

LATHA DEVI REPORT

Dr.(Mrs.) Sudershana Gujral
M.B.B.S D.G.O (Madras)

Res.& clinic
B 1/21, Vasant Vihar
New Delhi -5

Lata 42 years old housewife with 2 children. She underwent surgical operations like cholicystectomy, lords' operation, hysterectomy and appendisectomy during the period 1998 to 2003. In 2006 she again had pain in her pelvic region and on u/s a well defined mass was seen with in the wall of the rectum diagnosed as endometrosis and a specific medicine was prescribed to dissolve this eudometrioma . As she was so fed up after her previous ailments that she decided not to take any medicine and neither undergo any further investigation(like proctoscopy and MRI.)

During these days she came in contact with Yogi Ashwini . He assured her not to worry and told her certain Yogic exercises , asanas and Yogic kriyas . She says she has been doing all these regularly since 2006 and has no problem.

I am amazed to find that for the last 3 years she had no pain . How that mass disappeared without taking those specific medicines , I can only explain as her faith in her Guru and her following up of those practices in totality . His Divine power is the only evidence base proof or you may call it a miracle, Guru Kripa. She is actively involved in Dhyan Foundation work and I admire her stamina.

DR. Sudershanan Gujral

21 past tense, present perfect

GURUSPEAK

Manisha! I still remember the first time when I met her. She had practically come limping into the hall and sat down. Whenever I looked at her during the workshop on Sanatan Kriya, I saw just two big and beautiful eyes staring unblinkingly. I peeped into her life. She was a small child playing in the English countryside, a very happy and playful child; then suddenly there were sirens and a deafening sound and fire all around. The Nazi war planes were pounding the area. I heard her scream and her right leg got blown off. Then there were just screams and fire all around. I suppose her severe sciatica which apparently was just there was a past life impression which was carried forward by her soul.

Normally when the aura is cleansed by the practice of Sanatan Kriya most of the past life carry-forwards melt away... at least in her case they did melt away and she was cured, physically. Her emotional problems were the next to melt away. Today she is a healthy and happy person.

The color purple, radiant and glowing is therapeutic and at times powerful. If you keep staring at it, the colour has the warmth of red, yellow and blue hidden in it; somewhat mystical, intriguing and at some level, very calming. My Guru is violet and yellow. My Guru is golden and green. It is a feeling of bliss; a feeling of contentment; at times a feeling of being transformed, and transported to another realm.

Today I'm a different person. I met Yogi Ashwini seven years ago at the Hyatt in New Delhi. At that time my sciatica had made me immobile physically, and ill mentally. It seemed as if I had taken a plunge into a dark deep dungeon with no light in sight. However, Providence was kind and this feeling was to disappear in no time. Something remarkable happened.

A friend invited me to a Dhyan Foundation workshop. And that's where I met Yogi Ashwini. His presence was overwhelming. The next three days after meeting Him were trance like. I felt small and like a little child rattled off a list of problems. He just heard me out and nodded His head. I think I was ready to embark on this journey and had met this intriguing energy with a firm voice and magical incantations.

I had sciatica and was in deep excruciating pain. I could not walk or drive let alone run or simply get out of bed without help. And when I met Yogiji, I was initiated into a path of inner growth. Yogi Ashwini just asked me to close my eyes and be aware of His form. I could feel a golden light enveloping me. His technique worked wonders in a few days. My pain disappeared. The medication stopped. And I was up and about in no time. While I started walking with ease again my lifestyle and approach towards life and others changed. As I progressed professionally and materially, I became more aware. For the first time, I understood the meaning of service, of proper breathing and felt the vibration of *aum*. I felt the need for true internalisation and understood my role in the big scheme of things. And slowly but surely Yogi Ashwini moved into the Guru's space for me.

I had a dream since childhood which was unfulfilled, but within a short span of meeting Yogiji, I can say that its a dream come true, life is truly beautiful.

And today after about seven to eight years of my association with my Guru I can only say that *dhyan* and the *kriya* taught to me by my *Guruji* goes beyond a discipline, precincts of a country or mere *asanas* and a different technique. It's a foolproof science taught by a very gifted golden violet energy indeed. I am happy that I met Him and for all the experiences and learning *dhyan* has entailed. No matter where I go and how far I am from my Guru, his teachings are always with me.

Manisha Sethi

35 years, WRITER & GRAPHIC DESIGNER

22 from the clutches of evil to the bosom of divine

GURUSPEAK

Chhavi a very pretty and bubbly girl, I remember meeting her six years back in one of my sessions and there was an immediate connection. She was just there, not physically due to her job as a journalist, but I felt her presence at a much higher plane, which is beyond the scope of the five senses. Though physically I hardly saw her after that, but in the world of the ether she was always there.

Once again very sadly I need to mention here, the role of the dark forces of the nether world; you may also call it occult or black magic. There is a technique which black magicians use to slowly drain out the vital ***prana*** *from the body and replace it with heavy* ***prana****, this has the effect of giving the false impression of a disease but actually it is the immune system of the body which starts to fail and slowly the person starts to go weak and the immunity dips, contagious diseases take over the body and finally there is death.*

Who would do this dirty act with a girl like Chhavi is something which is beyond the scope of this book. I would like to mention, once more, that it has been proven that the dark forces are limited in their capacities and cannot complete their evil designs in the world of the Light ....in the realm of the Guru. Here I again offer my salutations to my Guru who intervened ....and Chhavi is normal today.........away and protected from such influences.

Miracles do happen. I have seen things changing and taking a complete U-turn. You may choose not to give up but at the same time you don't have much choice. You want to fight but you don't know what to fight. The sorriest state is the state of helplessness. I'm very close to my family (like most people). I have a younger sister who is like a child to me.

Everything in life was a smooth car ride, besides little speed-breakers. The path seemed clear but suddenly the road became rough and the car started making scary sounds. My 28-year-old sister started complaining of joint pains. But as always we believe nothing can go wrong with us. 'The other persons car can break down, mine is too new for any problems', is ones first thought. And then you are given a jolt to remind you, no one is an exception.

Things got more complicated. She had joint pains earlier, now it became worse. She started having problems doing routine work, like lifting a spoon. She had to sit for 10 minutes in the morning and hold herself before stepping into her shoes. Opening even a small bottle became tough. It was torture for her mind and body, and extremely painful for the entire family. We were concerned about her deteriorating health and felt even more helpless as we could not predict what new disaster was coming up next. Fear and anticipation of, when this invisible 'enemy' will hit hardest and from which corner it will spring upon us was trauma.

I must add here that my sister also has a child of her own who was only two years old then, and it was extremely disturbing to see the little kid suffer with the mother. This little child was much awaited, and therefore 'the apple of everyone's eyes'. The family wanted the best of everything for her. But all of us could see that the little one was being deprived of the very basic requirement of any child - mother's care.

My sister Chhavi's own parents-in-law are doctors, but still they could not elevate her pain. We thought of consulting a good orthopedic for second opinion, we consulted Dr. K N P Sinha (Rheumatologist), Max Hospital, Noida. The doctor got some tests done but could not really figure out much. Surprised, confused and to be precise frustrated; was our situation. First the doctor assured us it will be fine, but there was something he looked confused about, and later diagnosed the condition as rheumatoid arthritis. A condition where body's motor organs start to fail and slowly the condition deteriorates, till the person becomes a cripple and dies. There is no cure for such an ailment as is the case in all immunity disorders. We were shattered.

The doctor gave her a year or two to live. Seeing the condition she was in, her father-in-law a renowned doctor tried all kinds of treatments on her but she continued to deteriorate day by day. He tried every possible treatment, and it seemed clear by his words that we were going to loose her. He and his colleagues seemed to echo a consensus on this. I sought Yogi Ashwini's advice through my cousin Arti, who is an ardent student of Yogiji. He warned us that it could be fatal, but nonetheless Yogiji reassured us.

Chhavi's health was getting worse with every passing day. The pain that had begun from joints had moved to her lungs. She would cough uncontrollably, my ears would hurt and heart would be full of pain but I could not help her stop coughing. She would talk of dark figures moving around her and trying to hold her. She would get very

The doctor gave her a year or two to live. Seeing the condition she was in, her father-in-law a renowned doctor tried all kinds of treatments on her but she continued to deteriorate day by day.

frightened and we could not hold back our tears. After rheumatoid arthritis, doctors started testing her for tuberculosis.

Yogi Ashwini was always in touch and warned us that the situation is getting out of hands and it might get beyond repair. He said there is something which she is holding and that is killing her. We were surprised when Yogiji actually explained scientifically how her systems were failing and her immunity breaking down. He is not a doctor, but He knows everything. We cannot explain how, but what we know is that He was the only one who knew her exact condition in and out.

The specialist at the Apollo hospital said it was Sarcoidosis, an inflammatory disease that can affect almost any organ in the body, an immunity disorder, and there is no treatment for such an ailment. Every visitor and relative had a new solution to the soaring pain while she was getting worse day by day.

Nights were even tougher. My little sister could not sleep. I can never forget those three nights when sitting by her side I felt that this could be her last day. It was not just Chhavi suffering, the entire family was breaking down with the youngest daughter of the family suffering so deeply. The doctor now started testing for cancer, one felt helpless, blank, just didn't know what to do, where to get life from.

As a last resort, Chhavi went to meet Yogi Ashwini Himself. He explained to her the connection between her physical and emotional health. I had immense faith in Him and trusted Him. I knew that in the middle of this pathetic situation, Yogi Ashwini was there as a pillar of strength. That wonderful day Yogiji told us, nothing would happen to Chhavi.

The day Chhavi met Him I could see an immediate change in her. Yogiji assured her that she would come out of her misery sooner than expected. Within three days of meeting Yogiji, she was on her way to recovery. One day she smiled and said, "I don't feel the pain at all, see I can move my hands!" A change beyond logical explanation.

Meanwhile Chhavi also started going for Sanatan Kriya sessions regularly. Even though she could barely sit through the sessions, the change in her kept her motivated to go there regularly. I did my bit, family did its best but above all this effort, there was a force, par excellence; Yogi Ashwini who was working at a much higher level.

Her tests continued, the doctors were practically ready with the bad news, they moved to

Chhavi Golmei

biopsy. We saw the little girl of our family dressed in green gown moving with remorse and fear towards the operation lights. Only Yogiji's assurance kept 'hope' alive. Dr. Avdhesh Bansal, Indraprastha Apollo Hospital, performed the procedure of broncoscopy.

Yogiji had assured us that she was not suffering from cancer or even tuberculosis long before she underwent biopsy. After the biopsy, He said, "Chhavi is back, don't worry about the reports." With every iota of the fear that we experienced, our trust in Him grew. She went through the biopsy and the reports came. They were all negative. Thanks to Yogi Ashwini there was something else in store for Chhavi and us. A new life, a new beginning and a happy family. The reports stated that there was no - tuberculosis, no cancer!

Yogiji was there, strongly behind us. I suddenly saw Chhavi take a U-turn; we all noticed the transformation, the change. A painful body which had practically given up hope sprung back to

I am still bewildered as to what Yogi Ashwini did, how He did, but I know He got back my sister as He had promised.

life. We were overjoyed by this sudden improvement.

The miracle had happened. Complete recovery was a matter of days, that too without any medication. How her ordeal of few months ended in practically some days was a surprise to her and an unthinkable miracle to us. I am still bewildered as to what Yogi Ashwini did, how He did, but I know He got back my sister as He had promised. My father firmly believes in God, my mother prayed endlessly. I realized the Supreme Divine force; how it entered our lives and answered our prayers.

My kid sister is all aglow now, prettier and healthier than she ever was. There is a spring in her step and lightness in her every move. The glow on her face makes everyone disbelieve the fact that it was the same girl who was given only a couple of years to live by the medical fraternity.

We all knew the 'miracle' has happened. I can never express my gratitude in any possible form to Yogiji for this. It was not just about saving one life. It was bringing back 'life' to many lives. Thanks to Yogi Ashwini for everything.

Meenakshi Sharma

32 years, SR. JOURNALIST, STAR NEWS

23 death? you will have to wait!

GURUSPEAK

*Mohan, in an earlier life, was part of the Afghan invasions into India. I don't know how many times he has traveled the Hindu Kush range through the Khyber Pass. He was an ordinary **sawar** (mounted frontline soldier), who had spent nearly 150 years in looting and plundering innocent people.*

*At that time I had a small **ashram** on the foothills of the Hindu Kush range (I have spent two lifetimes in the service of mankind in those areas). I was atoning for the sins that I had committed in my previous seven lifetimes as a part of these invasions. Yes, I was also a part of these invasions for seven lives at a stretch!*

Every summer in the months from April to June, these soldiers would pass by for their regular plunders and I would sit under this huge Devdar, praying, that sense should prevail on these unfortunate people for like me, at this time, they do not know what they are sowing for themselves.

*It was the month of July. This group of around 500 **sawars** was moving uphill with their plunder when Mohan, with a group of around 10 **sawars**, came to my **ashram** with terrible injuries. He had suffered a lot of blood loss and his shoulder was nearly hanging out. I took him inside my hut and prepared bandages for his wound. His fellow **sawars** asked me if he would survive...I just looked at them for a few moments and then went inside, to do my treatment.*

He survived and within 15 days was fit for the journey back. Before leaving, he gave me his sword (there was a custom of giving your sword to someone whom you were indebted to and you were supposed to give the person what he desired in return for your sword). Those were violent times and life was highly uncertain; I smiled at him and gave his sword back and asked him to stay with me. He promised that he would come back next year and fulfill my wish...he and his friends then rode off. He did not come back the next year ....nor the year after... Mohan is back now to fulfill his promise, in this life.

I am Mohan and I am a clothing designer by profession. I have been with Yogi Ashwini for the last three years. I can't tell you how lucky and fortunate I consider myself for being with Yogiji.

Life is different when you are with your Guru. Just to stand next to Yogi Ashwini, every time puts me on to the path of experience and self realization. Every second of those years, or every breath that I have taken gave a new experience of how miraculous and Divine my Guru's abilities are.

It is difficult for me to put into words the enormity of what I experienced recently when I encountered a near death experience as the magnitude of the event is such that it left me in awe of Yogi Ashwini's powers. Yogiji not only brought me back to life but also made me a healthy and strong person within a week of this life threatening incident. How your Guru transfers *gyan* into you, in His own Divine ways even when you are not in a fully conscious state, is beyond my comprehension. But this is exactly what I experienced.

I've been an asthmatic since childhood. Although ever since I had met Yogiji, it had disappeared completely and I was leading an absolutely healthy life, till the time I chose to ignore His warnings and over worked myself. I started missing my regular Sanatan Kriya practice and my interaction with Yogiji.

On that fateful night I came back from work and felt a little uncomfortable while breathing. I took my inhaler and had my dinner and after that I do not remember anything. My physical memory was absolutely blocked. I woke up in the hospital room with my wife and family by my side. My wife told me softly "Mohan you had an asthma attack and you collapsed, everything is fine now". I was not able to feel anything. They were telling me what had happened; that I was in the I.C.U. and on the ventilator for three days and doctors had given only twenty percent chances of survival. Here's what happened in my wife's words...

"...On that fateful night after having dinner you went to bed and woke up suddenly feeling breathless. Even your inhaler did not help you breathe. You were soon gasping for breath. I rubbed your back but there was no relief. Agitated and helpless, you held on to the top of the door and started to jump in the hope of getting some breath back. I got scared and knew we had to go to the hospital, but you were feeling weak in the legs and could not walk. Even with my support you could barely drag yourself and by the time we reached the door, your legs gave way and you fell down and fainted. I immediately called Yogi Ashwini and told Him about the situation. He asked me to call the neighbours and to take Mohan, to the nearest hospital, informing me that he was reaching the hospital too. To my surprise our neighbour, Mr Mishra, DCP Logistics, Delhi Police, whom we had not met or talked with earlier, came to our help in the middle of the night and drove us to the hospital in his car. With the help of half a dozen people they carried you down from the first floor and to the hospital. It took around 20-25 minutes. You were taken into the emergency, your heart

I was circling around Him as He was creating spiral ripples around Himself and He was chanting some *mantra*.

rate was sinking and doctors had to artificially revive you. You had suffered hypoxia which the doctors told us later was a condition when the oxygen supply to the brain is stopped for some time due to shock or some other factor. You were taken to the I.C.U. and put on a ventilator. Doctors gave you 15-20% chance of survival..." I was too numb to understand what she was saying. For me this was all alien as I had no memory of that phase when I was unconscious, except for just one memory which seems to be from some other dimension.

My wife told me "Yogiji saved you". I closed my eyes. I knew where I had gone. I clearly remember an experience which is embedded in my memory like a painting on the wall. I had gone into a state of trance, which is a bit hard for me to explain. This happened when I was in the hospital and the doctors had given up on me. I was lying unconscious in the hospital. I experienced a state where there was nothing, only stillness, no body, no relationship, no environment, no sound, no colour, no vision, no taste. I had nothing- no religion, no time existed. I was just aware of my Guru's Divine form in which He was me and I was Him. There was no distinction, we were still. I was aware of Him, His energy form was creating an upward spiral, getting bigger as it moved up. I was circling around Him as He was creating spiral ripples around Himself and He was chanting some *mantra*. Amongst all this I could hear Him getting angry with me for ignoring His warnings and bringing myself to this state.

Since I came back to my senses, that is all that I can recall. I have no memory of how I suffered the asthma attack, when I collapsed, how I came to the hospital, what was going on around me and how I was brought into the ICU. The only memory I have is that of my experience with Yogi Ashwini in my unconscious state.

When I narrated this to my wife she was shocked. She said, "How come you know what Yogiji was doing when you were not in your senses?" She told me that during the time I was in the hospital in that state battling for my life, Yogi Ashwini was with her outside the hospital chanting *mantras*. He had said to her "Mohan is coming and going. I can feel him all around me... if he is still there he will not go anywhere. But you don't worry about anything". He was angry with me for dragging my own self to this state. Both of us were surprised as to how I knew exactly what Yogiji was doing, when I was lying unconscious in the ICU and when I had no other sensation, and Yogi Ashwini was, 'physically', outside the hospital.

Doctors cannot explain this. They were astonished. They are surprised and consider me a medical miracle and say so whenever they see me. They can't explain how I am alive with no brain damage in spite of no oxygen reaching the bloodstream for such a long period. But we know that it was Yogiji who got me back into the body, who gave me a new life and who was with me throughout, as not another being, but as me, taking me under His Divine protection. That's why I remember only Him and nothing else.

Interestingly an incident keeps coming to my mind, a question that I had asked my Guru a year back before this 'event'. One fortunate evening, I was with Yogiji and I asked Him, "What would happen if I have an accident and I survive but I lose my memory and I do not even recognize you or anybody else? Then what's Yog? What's this *kriya*? What's the purpose of life then?" He smiled at me in His mystical way, and then went into silence for a while. Later He said, "The purpose of life is just raising the level of your consciousness. That's it! I will tell you within a year what will happen if such a situation would arise..." and true to His words, this incident happened in the twelfth month after that dialogue.

Now after facing death I realise when there was nothing, nobody, no memory. My Guru was in His timeless form, which had no beginning and no end, no shape or size, and I recognised Him.

After a week of my ordeal, I went for my regular checkup. When my doctor was introduced to me (I'm using the word introduced, because I don't even remember his face), who had supposedly saved my physical body, told me that this is my new life, and I should take every step slowly like a baby. He was surprised at my recovery and remarked that I didn't look like the person who was in the ICU a week earlier. It seemed to him that I was coming straight from the gym; I was in such perfect condition. It is all because of Yogi Ashwini's grace and not just me but my entire family is indebted to Him. I can definitely say on this path of yog, I have taken one step towards my Guru.

32 years, FASHION DESIGNER

DISCHARGE SUMMARY

NAME	: MR.MOHAN SINGH	**Age/Sex**	: 32 Year(s) Male
UHID	: APD1.0000844365	**IPNO**	: 223445
Date of Admission	: 17-Apr-2009	**Date of Discharge**	:23-Apr-2009
Room/Ward	: 2523 (5th FLOOR T - I)		
Consultants			
1. Dr.CHAWLA RAJESH CHEST SPECIALIST		**Unit :RESPIRATORY**	

DIAGNOSIS :
Acute severe asthma
Post cardiorespiratory arrest

HISTORY:
Mr. Mohan Singh, 32-year old gentleman non smoker, non alcoholic, with history of bronchial asthma since childhood, was on asthalin inhaler, on SOS basis.
There is history of increased symptoms of breathlessness for last 1½ months, with increased frequency of asthalin use to 15-20 times a day. He was not on any oral medications.
On 17/4/09 early morning, he had increased symptoms and went into cardiorespiratory arrest at 3 am.
He was rushed to local hospital, was intubated and ventilated. ABG done there revealed a high PCO2 of 110.
He was shifted to IAH on ventilatory support for further care and management.

ON EXAMINATION:-
Conscious, oriented.
Afebrile
Pulse rate : 103/min
Blood Pressure : 134/ 79 mm Hg
Respiratory Rate : 17/min
No clubbing/ cyanosis/ pedal oedema/ icterus/ pallor/ lymphadenopathy.
Chest : Bilateral wheeze present
CVS : S1 S2 normal
No murmur/ rub/ gallop
P/A : Soft, no tenderness
Bowel Sounds +
No organomegaly
CNS : NAD.

COURSE IN THE HOSPITAL:-
He was admitted through triage in ICU under care of Dr.Rajesh Chawla (Sr.Consultant,

Contd ..2...

Respiratory and critical care medicine). Ventilatory support was continued, IV antibiotics, steroids, nebulisers and other supportive treatment was given. (antibiotics Augmentin, Levoflox). Initial labs revealed a Hb 14.7, TLC: 16000, urea: 22, Cr: 1.2, Na 137, K:4.4, platelets:2.94 L/cumm.

Blood gases were regularly done and he was gradually weaned off the ventilatory support. CXR-WNL.

There was an episode of hematuria and LMWH were held

Echo revealed EF 60%, no RWMA, good RV function.

He was successfully extubated on 18/4/09. BiPAP support was given keeping in mind the possibility of underlying OSA.

He showed gradual improvement. ABG (20/4/09) - 7.46/43.8/98.5/30.5/97.7.

PFT (22/4/09) suggestive of obstructive airways disease with significant response to bronchodilator.

S.IgE levels were done - report awaited.

Holter were done an empirical basis and revealed nil significant.

Sleep study is planned to be done later on OPD basis.

He is being discharged with following advice.

ADVICE ON DISCHARGE:-

Tab Wysolone 20mg once a day for 5 days
then 15 mg once a day for 5 days
then 10 mg once a day for 5 days
then 5 mg once a day for 5 days
then stop

Tab Pantocid 40mg once a day at 7am

Seroflo inhaler 205mcg 2 puff twice a day

Duolin inhaler 2 puff as and when required

Review with Dr.Chawla after one week in OPD

Kindly confirm your appointment with the OPD reception at 26925858, 26925801.

In case of emergency, please contact Casualty Medical Officer (CMO) on Tel. No. 26825558 (direct)/ 26925858 or 5801 on ext. no 2001 and 2012.

Should you require urgent advice on a medical problem viz

1. Fever of > 101.5 F / 38.6°C
2. Onset of new pain / worsening previous pain / chest pain/ breathlessness
3. Discharge from your operative wound.
4. Vomiting.
5. Any other complaint requiring immediate medical attention, please call the CMO

ALLERGIES :
Not known

Dr. CHAWLA RAJESH
SR.CONSULTANT
CHEST SPECIALIST

Registrar/Resident/C.M.O

Date : 23-Apr-2009 02:30 PM.

*DKP

India's First Internationally Accredited Hospital
Indraprastha Apollo Hospitals
Sarita Vihar, Delhi - Mathura Road, New Delhi - 110 076 (INDIA)
Tel. :91-11- 26925858, 26925801, Fax : 91-11-26823629, Emergency Telephone No. : 1066
Website : www.apollohospdelhi.com

SP

24 my celestial umbrella

GURUSPEAK

Nandini is much over 50 now, but is still able to hold ***asanas*** *like* ***Ardha Baddha Padmottan*** *or* ***Padhasta*** *or* ***Chakra*** *for close to half an hour, maintaining her pulse rate at 50 to 52. Developing this kind of control over her physical and emotional state in this short span of time that she has been with me is phenomenal.*

Yes it is definitely extraordinary. Yoga says that there are no miracles. Everything happens because of our past life ***karmas*** *and the grace of the Guru. Nandini's story is also one such revelation.*

I met her in my third previous life, where I was meditating in my ***ashram*** *in the desert areas of Bikaner. She was a famous dancer, and a very popular one too, who was involved with the commander of the king's army. One day I visited the court on an invitation, a child birth, and that was the first time I saw her perform and that was the first time she saw me. She was Nandini then, and is Nandini now.*

The very next day when I was going for my bath at 5 in the morning I saw her, waiting for me at the well. I knew that her quest had been awakened, but I was afraid her ***karmas*** *would hold her back. But for once she proved me wrong. She became my foremost disciple. And what happened to her suitor? Her present life husband, the gallant army officer who followed her here into this life, and, as their give and take exhausted, also left.*

I was born in a Bengali family in Kolkata, to parents who followed the path shown by Shri Ramakrishna Paramahansa Dev. Life was smooth and fine without any major ups and downs. 'Blind faith in Divine Energy', 'Work is Worship' and 'Service before Self' were the ethos I was driven by. I got married to an Indian army officer, and got absorbed in my family as a wife and mother. As a teacher, I was a friend, philosopher and guide, to a host of students over the years.

After living a life of a nomad for 20 years as an Indian army infantry officer's wife, we decided to settle in Delhi. The house we decided on was being constructed in Gurgaon. My husband was posted in an insurgency affected area of J&K. Our sons were studying and I was busy with my usual domestic and school responsibilities along with social commitments of life.

Suddenly, came a blow one fine morning in

2004, and a bolt of lightning that shattered everything in our lives. A message came that my husband had died in a firing incident and had become a martyr. The smooth surface of the ocean of my life became a rough turbulent sea that instant. I had no preparation for this impending doom.

With a big jolt, everything came to a halt for me. The house was not ready, children had their board exams, and their college education was yet to begin. There was unfinished work all around me. I felt completely helpless, without a protective shade on our head, and I could see nothing but darkness all around. My blind faith? !!... What happened to that?! Where was the blessing that sheltered me?!! . I was totally confused. My mind stopped working, and tears wouldn't stop rolling down. I developed an extremely negative attitude, with heavy emotional congestion, anger and hatred towards all… Depression, negative thinking, not being able to share others' happiness, no strength of bearing any responsibility, no physical strength - a complete 180 degree flip. I felt completely ruined. Everything in the surroundings that looked so beautiful to me earlier began to cause me pain. This abrupt end to my life of marital bliss made me an atheist. I stopped praying. There was no spiritual existence for me. Just complete darkness.

One day, Mrs. Singh, wife of Dr. Karni Singh, well known Neurologist with R & R Hospital, just asked me to go with her to Shri Aurobindo Ashram (where Dhyan Foundation classes were being conducted) and I accompanied her without knowing why I was going there. I just didn't hear what she had told me about Dhyan Foundation- maybe she didn't tell me anything. I am sure that in that state of mind, I wouldn't have gone with her if I was told that it was for yoga or to meet Yogiji. I was just not ready to take any advice or suggestion. But, a miracle happened, and the unique point is that I don't know exactly what, when, where, and how it happened!!! I saw Yogi Ashwini there.

I do not know what 'settled' deep inside me that day. Something happened in that first meeting which I cannot explain. I slept like a baby that night after many troubled sleepless nights.

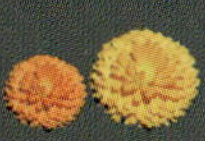

My friend asked me to talk toHim but I couldn't. I was choking, my thoughts were not clear. He looked at me, spoke to me and assured me that everything will be all right and will fall into place. I do not know what 'settled' deep inside me that day. Something happened in that first meeting which I cannot explain. I slept like a baby that night after many troubled sleepless nights. Inside, I felt washed and clean, no heaviness, no pain. After this meeting, every Sunday, I felt a compulsion to go there and listen to Yogiji and do whatever He said. I was not a competent driver, I did not know my way around, my sons worried about my Sunday evening trips to Dhyan Foundation, but come what may, I started going to class regularly just to get a *darshan* of Yogiji.

I will always be grateful to Dr. Karni Singh's wife for taking me to Yogi Ashwini.

There started my journey. Now I realise that miracles have been happening with me since the day I met Him. I single-handedly got the house ready to live in, got the sons going, continued school teaching and even took over as the India Operations Head of a US-based online education company. Where did I get all that physical and mental strength from? When did my thought process change? When did I start realising the concept of "Yoga" and "Guru" in its true sense? These are miracles which started happening immediately after I met Yogiji. All the issues of life have been taken care of; be it financial, administrative, my children's education or my son's job. Not a day have I felt helpless or alone after meeting Yogiji. His protective presence around me continues. Now my daily schedule consists of teaching Sanatan Kriya, educating under privileged children, working for examville.com (the company, I work for), running a learning center and I am also an executive member of the Managing Committee of our society. People say to me, "You look so young for your age; there is a glow on your face. You are so calm and composed and there is a kind of attraction in you. How do you handle so many activities in life so aptly and effectively". How do I do these things? Simple, with Yogi Ashwini's boundless energy.

Somewhere inside me I strongly feel that I had some connection with Yogi Ashwini even before I met Him. Life has become meaningful and purposeful. Now I have no regrets, no remorse, no heaviness. I can now laugh again, and be positive in all my dealings and interactions. This transformation is a unique miraculous experience for me. To be pulled out of crippling pain like this and be moulded into a spiritually useful member of society and Dhyan Foundation.

Nandini Ghosh

52 yrs, ALL INDIA OPERATIONS HEAD, EXAMVILLE.COM

25 permanently protected

GURUSPEAK

Mr. Aggarwal has actually completed the basics of ***kundalini*** *awakening under Guru's grace in his past three lives. The basic levels take a* ***sadhak*** *till the* ***anahat chakra****, after the* ***anahat,*** *the journey of the spirit becomes a little difficult.*

As he had lots of physical desires still left in him, hence such a late awakening of the ***antahakarna*** *in this lifetime. His son merely became the instrument for him to locate me once more so that his awakening could be culminated into the final journey and so the final journey. I am not allowed to comment on the state of his* ***kundalini*** *in this book, but can just give the indication that this possibly might be his last birth in the present* ***mahayug****.*

My son Vipin joined Dhyan Foundation in the month of August 2006, after seeing an episode from the serial '*Mano Ya Na Mano*' on television. I joined in December the same year and feel my search for a spiritual anchor is over.

I want to share two incidents that shook me up, yet I was unharmed. The date was 20/2/2007, I was returning from Khairthal (District Alwar) to Delhi. I was travelling by taxi. We were near Tizara at around 8-9 pm. I was drowsy and was drifting in and out of sleep after a long and tiring day.

Just then, with a jolt I was thrown towards the front seat. I heard the tyres screeching, and a loud thud and the car swerved sharply to one side. Simultaneously, I saw a flash of white hit the windscreen and then get flung out towards the road. My first thoughts were we were overturning. The car seemed to have tilted to one side on two side wheels. I heard myself shouting at the driver.

As soon as the car stopped, my driver and I rushed out to see what had happened. Everything happened so fast that our brains did not register what had 'hit us'. My heart was pounding, as I looked into the darkness. Other than our car headlights, the road was absolutely dark. I saw a bike lying on the ground, and two people lying on the road, away from each other.

And that is when I figured out that two boys riding on a bike had crossed the road all of a sudden, from left to right in the dark and the driver had applied brakes with full force, but could not avoid the collision. One of the boys had rolled onto the bonnet because of the impact and smashed into the windscreen. One boy was badly hurt and could not walk and another had minor injuries. He stood up

and started walking. I picked up the boy with severe injuries and decided to go to Tizara Hospital and get him patched up. By this time their family members had arrived at the spot.

Horror stories of mob violence rushed through my mind. But I stood there, knowing that we had not done anything wrong. Around 50-70 villagers gathered on that spot but nobody blamed us. Instead, they kept saying that this particular spot is prone to accidents. Also they felt the fault was of the negligent boys, who crossed the road without looking for oncoming traffic in the darkness. We took the boys to the hospital where they were treated. After settling the matter, we drove off and I thanked Yogi Ashwini, as, because of His grace we came home without even a scratch on our body and no ill feelings between us and the villagers. It was indeed no less than a 'miracle'.

In this day and age, when 'road rage' is so common and so lethal, we had an 'experience' which left us shaken but safe. At about 8 pm, one evening, on the way back from an event near Mehrauli in New Delhi, all of a sudden a motorcycle screeched and stopped my car. Two well built local boys were on it. One of them was in a very angry mood, looking for a fight. He was hurling abuses and waving his arms in the air. He glared at us with bloodshot eyes. My heart missed a beat. I quickly connected with Yogiji from my *anahat*. Yogiji's image appeared in front of me. I looked into his merciful eyes and prayed silently. Seconds later, I confidently rolled the window down and asked the youth very politely, "What happened?" He suddenly cooled down and said, "ok, go ... " and they went away quietly as if nothing had happened. My wife and I were stunned. Only Yogiji could have protected us like this from those aggressive young men bent on violence.

On a deeper level, I have become much calmer; my own outbursts are now a thing of the past. My awareness has increased tremendously and I now willingly participate in service. All these welcome and much-needed changes are a blessing from Yogi Ashwini.

I want to share with all one of my wife's experiences on her behalf. Santosh suffered from back problems since 1977, we tried each and every cure available, but to no avail. Then on that wonderful day in 2009, when Yogiji conducted a workshop on spine and back problems, my wife's suffering came to an end. She was instantly relieved of her pain. I have no words to describe this 'miracle' and its impact on our lives. I can only thank the Divine over and over again for making me meet Yogi Ashwini.

Nanak Chand Aggarwal

59 yrs, ASST. GEN. MNGR, DCM SRIRAM CONSOLIDATED LTD

MRI & SPIRAL CT SCAN CENTRE

38, PKT. C-9, SEC-8, (NEAR MADHUBAN CHOWK) ROHINI, DELHI-85
PH: **27940623, 27942624, 27945847, 27945848** FAX: **27940474**

NAME	:	Mrs. Santosh	AGE	:	55Yrs
SEX	:	Female	DATE	:	14.02.05
REF. BY	:	Dr. M.S. Aggarwal			

MRI LUMBO SACRAL SPINE

MRI of Lumbo - Sacral Spine was performed using T1 W Axial & Sagital, T2 W Axial & Sagital sequences. MR Myelogram was also performed using Sagital and Coronal sequences.

There is normal curvature and alignment of lumbar spine.

Vertebrae are normal in height and signal intensity.

Marginal osteophytes at L3, L4 and L5.

There is loss of signal intensity on T2W sequences at D9-10,L3-4, L4-5 and L5-S1 intervertebral disks suggestive of dessication.

Rest of intervertebral disks are normal in height and signal intensity.

Mild diffuse diskal bulges are seen at L3-4 and L4-5 levels indenting the thecal sac.

No other significant diskal bulge / herniation is seen.

Mild facet joint arthrosis is seen at L4-5 level with associated facet joint effusion and ligamentum hypertrophy causing posterior indentation of thecal sac.

Lower dorsal cord and conus medullaris are normal in calibre and signal intensity

No evidence of pre / paravertebral collection is seen.

IMPRESSION

- Mild diffuse diskal bulges at L3-4 and L4-5 levels indenting the thecal sac and ligamentum flavum hypertrophy with facet joint arthrosis at L4-5 level causing posterior indentation of thecal sac.
Please Correlate Clinically

DR. MOHIT GUPTA
RADIOLOGIST

Not valid for medicolegal purpose
It is only a professional opinion and not the diagnosis, should be correlated clinically and with other investigations.

MRI (OPEN HIGH GRADIENT) • CT SCAN (FAST SPIRAL) • MAMMOGRAPHY • ULTRASOUND • X-RAY (500MA) • ECG, EMG, EEG (18 CHANNEL) • ECHO WITH COLOUR DOPPLER STUDIES • EXERCISE & DOBUTAMINE STRESS ECHOCARDIOGRAPHY • FETAL & PAEDIATRIC ECHOCARDIOGRAPHY • UMBILICAL BLOOD FLOW STUDIES • PULMONARY FUNCTION TEST • PERIPHERAL VASCULAR STUDIES, CAROTID, UPPER LIMB, LOWER LIMB • TMT & 24 HOURS HOLTER MONITORING

AN ISO 9001 : 2000 CERTIFIED LABORATORY

26 journey of a hunter to a sadhika

GURUSPEAK

Nitasha, a very talented painter by profession, who is a grandmother now, is one of the brightest teachers at Dhyan Foundation. Wherever there is a problem group of students, she is sent there and within minutes she has the whole group nodding their heads in approval.

In her previous births, her life has been one of extravagance and of plenty, soaked in luxury. She never thought of charity or service, just luxuries for herself.

I need to mention one specific lifetime of hers where she was a minister in the court of the King of Alwar (about 300 years back in time) and was very fond of tiger hunts. She (who was then a man) used to accompany the king religiously. I happened to meet her (him) in one of these hunts. The sun was setting and the preparations for the hunt were underway; a goat was being tied to a tree as bait and a ***machan*** *(elevated hunting platform) was being built on a nearby* ***bargad*** *(banyan) tree. This was the very place which I would visit in the evenings for my* ***sandhya*** *rituals. Seeing me approach, she (he) walked towards me and requested that I take what I require and go away fast as a tiger was expected. I smiled at him and said that this is the place for my* ***sandhya*** *and no tiger will come here, so they should not waste their time and go somewhere else; he insisted on being there and so did I. I sat under the tree and they made their preparations for the* ***machan*** *on another tree.*

I sat throughout the night under the tree and they kept their vigil on the ***machan****. Nothing happened; disappointed, in the early hours of morning, they came down from the* ***machan*** *and asked me why I spoilt their hunt. I told them that it was not a good thing to do and in my presence the tiger would not come. They insisted that it was a coincidence and the tiger would come the next night for the goat, as this place was known for tigers. I just smiled and went away.*

This continued for the next six nights. I used to sit under the tree and they would wait on. After six nights he came to me and asked for an explanation; I told him that I will explain but in another lifetime when he would be prepared to listen... I think 'he' finally is listening.

Many of us have this fascination for stone rings recommended by god-men for a better future. Till about five years ago, I was no exception to this rule. I used to wear several rings on my fingers. Rings of stones that were supposed to 'elevate' my position. But as time passed, the stones became a sort of psychological support for me. I felt dependent on them for my wellbeing. I was a prisoner, a slave, to these coloured stones.

When I joined the Foundation four years ago, I realized that suddenly my rings of blue, topaz, ruby and pearl were all dust compared to what my Guru, Yogi Ashwini had bestowed on me. He never asked me to remove them or stop wearing them, as He never stops anyone from doing anything... Just being with Him, made me experience the uselessness of the rings I wore. They lost their shine and I took them off… just like that.

Yogi Ashwini monitors every second of my existence; every thought, every action is in His purview. He extended his continuous presence into my being, deep into my soul. The difficulties that plagued me became insignificant. Interestingly when I joined, He had asked "How do you make a line which is drawn, small? " I had no answer. He said, “Draw a line bigger, than the previous one, next to it". He did exactly that for me. He soaked me completely into the Guru energy. And all my problems, all my difficulties became trivial compared to the sense of continuous protection I started feeling. On the first day itself, he said to me, 'Your experience will be immediate.' I listened to Him with a blank mind... That night I sat down to do Sanatan Kriya and realized what He meant. With my eyes closed, in a dark room, I saw His full form as it is in the physical, like a colour photograph. I was stunned.

Soon after I joined, my husband had to undergo an investigative surgery for his cholesterol. My husband, children and I were extremely tense. That day, the doctors started the investigative surgery to decide about the bigger operation. The surgical procedure was on, and I ran to Yogiji's office. Emotionally, I was shattered due to the stress of this 'test'. I just broke down; Yogi Ashwini looked at me like a father and said, “Go, nothing is wrong with him”. Overjoyed, I rushed back to the hospital and saw my husband laughing and joking. The doctors informed us that there was no need for the heart surgery. I was amazed how the doctors who, till a couple of hours back were pushing us to go for the heart surgery, now said that my husband was fine. Thanks to Yogi Ashwini, weeks of intense agony just vanished away that instant. We came home from the hospital like a happy family.

Nitasha Jaini

46 years, FREELANCE VISUAL ARTIST

Preet Gynae & Medical Clinic

– Medical services for the whole family –

Dr. P. S. Ahluwalia
M.B.B.S. (Gen. Physician)
MCI Regd. # 11757 DMC Regd. # 11145
Ex. Resident Medical Officer (Medicine)
› **Sir Ganga Ram Hospital**, New Delhi
› **Jaipur Golden Hospital**, Rohini, Delhi
Medical Officer: **State Bank of India**
On Panel of : **S.B.I., Univ. of Delhi**

Dr. (Mrs.) Harpreet Ahluwalia
M.B.B.S. (Gynae & Obst.)
RMC Regd. # 016580 DMC Regd. # 10939
Ex. Medical Officer:
E.S.I. Hospital, New Delhi
On Panel of : **Univ. of Delhi**
Kendriya Vidyalaya

TO WHOM-SO-EVER IT MAY CONCERN

This is to state that Mrs Pooja Bharija aged 31 yrs was suffering from Left Lower leg varicose veins from the last 6 yr i.e since 2003. She was on regular NSAID's + stockings.

From the last 1yr she has shown marked improvement and she is asymptomatic after taking treatment from Sanatan Kriya Dhyan foundation as stated by the patient. She is able to perform her regular activities + daily routine now i.e since 1year and is not taking any medicines

Dr. (Mrs.) Harpreet Ahluwalia
M.B.B.S.
RMC Regd # 016580 DMC Regd. # 10939

Timings : 7.00 AM to 9.00 AM 9.00 PM to 10.00 PM SUNDAY CLOSED

B-42, New Krishna Park, Janak Puri West Metro Stn., New Delhi - 110 018, Ph.: 2551 3153

Not Valid for Medical Legal Purpose

27 magic of one look

GURUSPEAK

Pooja is a very vibrant and dynamic lady. She has great expectations from life and her family. When a person has so much dynamism inside, it is indicative of a storehouse of ***pranic*** *energy; actually, has it in excess would be the right way to put it. When this happens, the body is not able to adjust to this excessive force and gets overheated. The result, an ailment manifests.*

Actually when one faces disappointments in life from near and dear ones, and one is not under the grace of a Guru, then these disappointments turn into emotional blocks. ***Pranic*** *blocks or congestions would be the right word. The aura which normally ought to have lighter colour shades now turns heavy and dark, like when you add black to let's say yellow; what results is a dirty brown.*

Something similar happens to a person's aura. This dirty brown is indicative of disease due to emotional congestions, in spite of having a high supply of ***pranic*** *energy. In her case, I requested my Guru to remove the black to as great an extent as possible. I think my call was answered and what happened after that is best told in her words...*

I developed varicose veins in 2003 during my 2nd pregnancy. I had twins. The problem was in my left leg. The pain was unbearable, and I was slowly slipping into depression, as I thought that I would have to live with this problem throughout my life. I could not give time to my kids and was unable to stand for more than 10 minutes. I was perpetually on painkillers and this constant and prolonged pill-popping was having an adverse effect on my stomach. My foot used to remain swollen and the doctor said that I would have to get an operation done and wear stockings all my life. Then, as luck would have it, more than a year ago, I heard about Dhyan Foundation and had the chance to meet Yogi Ashwini. I informed Him about the problem and broke down, lamenting and wondering if I would ever be able to go back to a normal life. He smiled and had a very comforting expression in His eyes. He just asked me to stand straight and stay connected with Him. He glanced over me once and I could feel some tingling

sensation in my legs. Then He just looked in another direction and told me to inform Him if the problem persists. Till the time I reached home, the tingling sensation continued. I had my dinner and went to sleep. The next morning I realized that the pain was 50% less. I could not believe that this had actually happened. Within days my problem just disappeared, never to come back again! There is no need for any surgery and I have thrown away those ugly stockings. I'm enjoying my motherhood to the hilt and doing all household chores without any fear of the pain. I have stopped taking all those horrible painkillers because of my Guru's grace. I thank Him a thousand times. His words, "Guru is an experience, not an intellectual understanding", now make perfect sense to me.

Pooja Bhairja

He glanced over me once and I could feel some tingling sensation in my legs. Then He just looked in another direction and told me to inform Him if the problem persists.

31 years, HOMEMAKER

nothing is a coincidence

GURUSPEAK

Some people evaluate evolution with a measuring tape. They want results and they want instantaneous results; otherwise they are disappointed.

Rajan is one of those kinds. Since his wife was involved in so much social work with the Foundation, the house began to get disturbed; he regularly used to ask her, "What value have you added to the family today?" Being a marketing person, input and output should be tangible, to the extent that he should consider it tangible. It became so bad that one day she expressed her inability to continue with the good work. I had to interfere by helping her encash some of her good ***karmas*** *instantly. I requested my Guru to make her husband happy, so that her path is not disturbed.*

It is well said that on an empty stomach you cannot think about God. Even if God comes in front of you, you will ask for what you understand, and that is food. The whole essence of life will evade you. I had to make him happy. I am glad that he is happy today and she is progressing on the journey of the spirit.

Yogi Ashwini had an immediate impact on me; this was obvious within hours of seeing Him. To explain further, since I work in the media marketing business, I had met an MNC client in the morning who'd asked me not to bother her again. She'd just brushed me off and told me that she would call me if a requirement came up. I was dejected and depressed. All my efforts were not yielding results, in spite of my repeated attempts. That afternoon I happened to meet Anu Kalra, an old friend of mine. I shared this issue with her, as she is also in media like me. She suggested that if it was okay with me, I accompany her that very day for a *dhyan* session. I met Yogiji for the first time that day. Later, when I came back to my car and switched on my mobile phone, I had a missed call from the same client. I called her; it was well past 10pm. She wanted the rates, and was ready to start business immediately. Next morning, I got her bookings for the 'daily' I work with. This definitely cannot be a mere coincidence, for otherwise, why did it not happen earlier? At that point, a part of my logical brain told me that it was a coincidence, but ever since, too many positive coincidences have been happening.

After that, such happenings at regular intervals have become routine. I know in my heart that Yogiji knows when I need help and He helps me without being asked. Being in sales, there are days when I wander like a lunatic in the heat of Delhi, with little to show for my efforts and reach office disappointed. But to my surprise, there are bookings that have come in from

some client, who I met long back and I have new business. My day gets rewarded. Yogiji's invisible hand holds me and is always there for me.

Moreover, time taken to achieve results has reduced considerably, which is unbelievable but true, thus increasing my productivity and leading to better professional recognition. I am consulted on all major company initiatives and my advice is sought after in complicated cases.

My achieving financial stability is totally because of Yogi Ashwini. I see a decent balance in my account that gets enhanced as I earn incentives due to my increased productivity. I often exceed my sales targets. Freedom from financial worries leads to inner peace and better concentration levels and of course, better living.

My achieving financial stability is totally because of Yogi Ashwini

Moreover industry recognition has also come in. I have been invited by a management institute to be part of their visiting faculty. Though I have been associated with this institute in the past, they never invited me as faculty. This is a new development that happened only last week. Teaching youngsters is a fun-filled option. It could well be a future career option after I retire. This is rare and special and definitely Yogiji's blessing; as there are more qualified persons available in the industry; but not everyone is blessed with the *sanidhya* of Yogiji. I can safely tell you now, that nothing that has happened to me was a mere 'coincidence'.

P. Rajan

44 years, CHIEF MANAGER, MIDDAY IINFOMEDIA LTD

29 healing touch

GURUSPEAK

Ranjana and Rear Admiral Byce are a couple with a typical armed forces background; simple, trusting and widely travelled... something like the 'been there, done that' types.

*In the first meeting itself, I knew that here was a couple who would have their first experience of the spiritual world very fast. When they first met me, they described to me that, how they had travelled the whole globe and met so many so-called Gurus and tried out a plethora of **kriyas** and techniques, but all were a waste.*

*I still remember Rear Admiral Byce telling me that how when he was the military attaché posted in the US, he would meet a new yoga Guru nearly every second day and how these 'Gurus' were fooling the world and bringing a bad name to the subject of yoga. I had just smiled at him at that time and told him that the problem was **maya**. Obviously someone who is himself tied with **maya** cannot open your bindings. His prompt reply was that I have yet to see an organization which does not charge. I again smiled and told him that now you have come to one, let's see what happens.*

What happened thereafter has been described by Ranjana for the reader... Such is the power of yoga.

I along with my husband met Yogi Ashwini a few years back. In this life-altering meeting, I got to experience a fraction of what Yogiji is. The stance and power of His presence was remarkable. He exuded energy and peace. Those days I used to have pain in the knees, spondylitis, and continuous back pain. I told Yogiji about these difficulties. Yogi Ashwini smiled and said, "Turn around", I was a little surprised but I obediently turned around. I felt the slightest feather like touch at the nape of my neck. Yogiji again said, "Turn back." I turned back to face Him. I looked at Him with questions in my eyes. He just smiled and said, "Let's see, what happens" and started talking to some other people present. Later, while walking towards the car, I noticed lightness in my body; a deep sense of relaxation and well being enveloped me. I could not understand it there and then. The next morning when I got up, the realization hit me. My back pain and spondylitis had disappeared. I witnessed a 'miracle' first hand. I was on cloud nine. I instantly knew my 'problems' were over. My faith became deeper and more connected with the Divine than ever before. Even the doctors at the R & R Hospital could not explain this sudden recovery.

One more astonishing incident comes to my mind. Tarana, my grand daughter, was just 2 weeks old when she developed an eye infection. My daughter and son-in-law showed her to a doctor who gave her some eye drops. Tarana was all right for a few days. However, the infection recurred soon thereafter and this time the eye-lid was almost shut. We were all very worried, and my daughter sought an appointment with the child specialist.

My faith and connection with Yogi Ashwini was so strong that I felt Yogiji Himself was with me

Same evening I was sitting in *dhyan* as taught by Yogi Ashwini. As soon as I got up from my *dhyan*, I took Tarana in my lap. My faith and connection with Yogi Ashwini was so strong that I felt Yogiji Himself was with me, and I started doing 'healing' on Tarana, although I have not yet learnt healing. I just did the *Guru Vandana, Ganeshji's* invocation, *Shri Maha Mritunjaya* chant; I sent red, green and then blue light into the eyes of the baby, and concluded this *kriya* with *Guru Vandana*.

The very next morning everybody was delighted and amazed. There was no trace of infection in the baby's eyes. And once more the doctor could not explain this .We all sent Yogiji a silent thank-you.

54 years, HOMEMAKER

Ranjana Byce

30 faith can move mountains

GURUSPEAK

Reena, when I first met her, gave the feel of being a very basic person. Her aura could be categorized as a very basic aura with the usual normal shades of greens, oranges and blues. Nothing extraordinary or phenomenal about her; just a normal housewife whose basic concern was her husband, her children and her source of income. I used to earlier believe that miracles happen with only those who command superior auras and are a little removed from the merely normal, but Reena proved me wrong. Her strong faith actually moved mountains for her...It is a practical case of moving mountains by just faith - faith in the Guru.

Meditation or *dhyan* for me was something that only yogis or people who had troubled lives practiced. I was introduced to yoga at a workshop held by the Dhyan Foundation at the Regent Hotel in Dehradun. I learnt for the first time that yoga was not just physical exercises but a much deeper concept, actually not just a deep concept but, as Yogi Ashwini says, "Yoga is the final frontier."

How life takes a positive turn the day you meet your Guru, is remarkable. It is to be experienced and I'm sharing this experience to make people believe that miracles do happen even in today's world. I realize that it is very important to have the protection and guidance of a Guru and the knowledge that I have, a guide who protects me against all harm, gives me a lot of confidence.

A mother worries mostly for her children, her home, husband and family. Like all mothers, I was worried about my children's future especially for my son's, who was very playful but in spite of being intelligent, did not perform as well as he should have. My other great worry was about my husband, who was addicted to drinks and was least inclined to give it up. Surprisingly, both my worries were taken care of by Yogiji. Just because of a passing mention by me. I informed Yogiji about the reason of my anxiety and depression. Yogi Ashwini said, "No one is happy with what they have, but I don't see any reason for you to worry. Everything seems to be perfect in the near future." I just clung on to those words and within a month, my son got campus placement in a reputed company even before he appeared for his graduation examinations. By Yogi Ashwini's grace, my husband gave up drinking completely, without us coaxing him or him having to make any effort. He just started feeling sick of having those drinks which were his life! Believe it or not, 'just like that'!

There are other blessings, like having enough

money for my requirements, even for travelling. There is also help at hand, whenever I need it. Things settle down suddenly and unexpectedly to suit me. My prayers are always answered. In this age, when people with ailments are not encouraged to work, the management at my place of work (a school) is very caring and considerate towards me. Life is still full of challenges and problems but I have stopped worrying about them as I know that everything will be sorted out. Such is the power of Yogi Ashwini.

Reena Dangwal

56 years, TEACHER, CONVENT OF JESUS & MARY

31 divine visions

GURUSPEAK

The soul resides in the body and is to be awakened from its dormant states. Once there then the body experiences the world of the spirit. Its not the eye which sees, its not the ear which hears, its not the tongue that speaks. When you connect with your Guru then the meaning of these words dawns on you. You see with eyes closed and hear what no one else can. And speak the words which you never knew. This is one such case where the body is experiencing the higher dimensions of Creation.

I joined National Association for the Blind in 2008, I was twenty three years old . My life was full of tears, I have no memory of my parents, I have been brought up by my late grandfather, and now my uncle and his wife are my legal guardians. Life was never easy, but it took a turn for the worst when I had an accident in class eight, and lost my sight completely.

I used to cry myself to bed every night, emotionally I was a wreck. In NAB I was introduced to the Sanatan Kriya, which has been formulated by Yogi Ashwini . I had the good fortune to meet Him also. And soon after meeting Him I saw the image of Lord Ganesh, I was totally taken aback when the image appeared before my eyes. I had not seen any thing with my eyes for a long time. Soon my sleep improved and my emotions also balanced out. I started feeling more secure and confident. Some weeks later I was blessed with an image of someone sitting in front of me with his hair tied in a knot on his head and a snake around his head. I have also seen colours like silver, red. Once I saw a vision of someone wearing a red *chunni* in my *dhyan*. I was never told about such images by the Dhyan Foundation volunteer who taught me the *kriya*. I was never asked to visualise them, there were no suggestions made, and I don't know from where these visions came and what they mean, but the change in me is welcome and life enhancing.

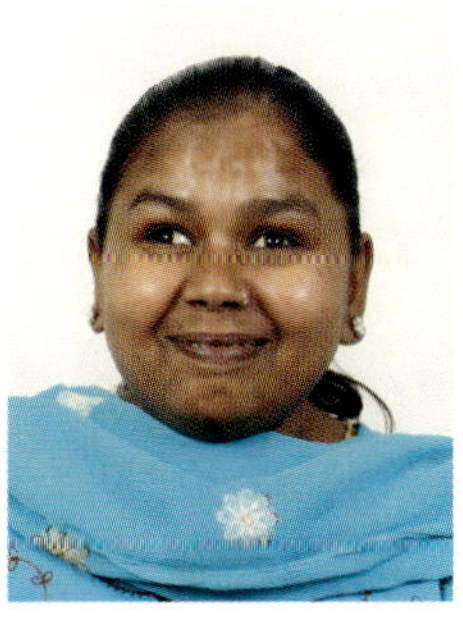

These images have reaffirmed my faith and given me the confidence of knowing that I am at the right place with the right Higher being, Yogi Ashwini .

Reena Das

24 years, NAB STUDENT

A-520, Sushant Lok - I,
Gurgaon - 122 002.
Phone : +91 - 124 - 4041288 / 89, 4042266, 2385657 / 58.
Fax : +91 - 124 - 4041286.
Mobile : +91 - 98186 44599, 98186 46155.

(3)

UMKAL HOSPITAL
More then just care...
An ISO 9001 : 2000 Certified Hospital

OPD CARD

Date	18/Sep/2008 12:42	Patient No	P0910328
Reg No	OC0901760	Age/ Sex	46 Yrs/ F
Patient Name	Ms. RENU RUKHI	Phone	9810108018
Address	C- 363C ,SUSHANTLOK - 1 GGN	Department	ENT
Consultant	DR. LALIT KOCHHAR (MBBS, MS (DOMS))		9810344429
Timings	MON, THU 10 - 1 PM.		

18/9/08

C/o pain & Discharge Lt-Ear

S/o. Tympanoplasty Lt Ear 1 1/2 yr back

. Cold cash.

OE

perforation with thick Discharge

Nose DNS with evidence of Sinusitis

Throat congested

Xray PNS water view

PTA S R Ophthalms Sector 14 market. Narendra Sharma 40818450 Monday 11 Am

Rx

Tab Distaclor 500 1 TDS x 5 dy

Tab Rupanex 1 OD x 5 dy

Duonase nasal spray Two puffs each nostril twice daily

Genticyn HC Ear drops 2-3 drops TDS x 5 dy

Karvol plus steam inhalation twice daily.

Tab Combiflam 1 BD x 3 dy.

EMERGENCY HOTLINE : 41 00 000

32 pursuit of happiness

GURUSPEAK

*Renu is amongst those people who come with a phenomenal storehouse of **prana** because of their past life **karmas**. They are blessed with everything possible which the physical life has to offer but because of the veils of ego and the **karmic** dust which their **antahkarna** has gathered, they are unable to see the true purpose of life and not just that, they are unable to enjoy the various blessings given to them by the Divine. They waste their life in useless social pursuits and are always chasing their false egos and are unable to enjoy this life.*

All that my Guru did was removed that dust, rest whatever happened..........

I joined the Foundation about two years ago. My husband is a Captain in the merchant navy; as a result he comes home for 2 months and is sailing for 4. I was very concerned that my joining the Foundation would irk him, and I would face some opposition. But a 'miracle' happened when he did not react unfavourably. In fact, may be he noticed that everything around me was in a better state. The tension in the house is remarkably reduced, and the atmosphere is of well being and happiness.

As my husband is not home for long periods, I used to get very hassled by the day to day problems of life; now these very problems seem to solve themselves. Every difficulty dissolves and disappears on its own.

When I met Yogi Ashwini, at that time I used to get a 'discharge' from the left ear. I got surgery done, but it had made no difference. One day I took my problem to Yogiji. He gave a very surprising reply to me, He said, "Ok, I'll talk to the doctor". I was confused, as I thought, may be, I would have to give the doctor's name and phone number to Yogi Ashwini. I was very unsure. Then out of the blue, just like that, the discharge stopped. It was just not there. Immediately, I understood that Yogiji, by His presence had just 'healed' me. He had obviously 'talked to the highest doctor ever'. I could not believe that I was a recipient of 'miracle healing'. Yet, that is what it was.

One day I thought to my self, my spiritual growth is not 'happening'. I shared this with Yogi Ashwini. And lo and behold, the biggest miracle was awaiting me. The next day itself, I saw, Guru Nanak Devji, standing right in front of me, in a dream which left me spellbound. When I got up, I knew Yogiji had once again given me my answer without saying a word.

Earlier I used to loose my temper over small

insignificant events, but now my temper is a thing of the past.

I and my family have received innumerable blessings from Yogiji who has taken on the 'responsibility' of innumerable people in every aspect of existence.

Renu Rekhi

The next day itself, I saw, Guru Nanak Devji, standing right in front of me, in a dream which left me spellbound

47 years, HOMEMAKER

33 implausible ...possible

GURUSPEAK

Ridhi, is the name of the consort of Lord Ganesha and is indicative of pleasures and good health with fulfillment of worldly desires, for her and for those who come in contact with her.

But contrary to her name, the description that her mother was giving to me was just the opposite. I still remember her mother describing the long medical history and the plethora of problems that they were going through... I was listening... and not listening... as images of her as a middle-aged woman wearing a bright red dress, a long traditional skirt with a short top, in the deserts of Rajasthan, flashed in my mindscape. She, in her fourth past life seemed to be administering something to a child, looked like the son of her co-wife, and then the child began throwing up as she left the room in a hurry... I knew the exact reason for her problem. I began petitioning Lord Ganesha... what followed is given here in Ridhi's own words.

When you meet your Guru, experiences happen from the first day. They may not seem apparent, but sooner or later you realize what is happening to you. They range from the trivial, like getting out of an unhealthy relationship or moving away from friends that were a bad influence on you or even getting a beautiful glow, to something greater, like finding meaning and purpose in life, breezing your way through work, losing several kilos and leaving diseases behind.

Then, of course, there are experiences of the subtler dimension which not only change your outlook towards life but also your shape and form. Or experiences with the supernatural which leave you flummoxed. All this and more has happened to me.

I am a journalist and before meeting Yogi Ashwini, I did not believe in para-phenomenon, as too many times in my career I have seen the 'so called *babas*', literally beg and cajole journalists to write about them in the media. Having seen too many frauds in my career, I just kept away from information which bordered on the 'impossible'. Fortunately, when I saw Yogi Ashwini for the first time, He was wearing blue jeans, sneakers and a simple T shirt. I somehow related to Him immediately. He spoke in English and explained everything like a science professor. The experience I am mentioning here is perhaps one that everyone can easily relate to as it is the most physical of my experiences so far.

Two years ago, I fell seriously ill. I had 104 degree temperature which vehemently refused to come down. My father is a Brigadier and a doctor and like any good doctor he made me undergo various tests. All tests showed that everything was normal. My body seemed to be functioning fine, barring a few inflamed cells/organs. Medicine, I realized operated on assumptions and a number of hit-and-trials. The best doctors of the Army were at my disposal. Several blood tests later, when they still could not decipher what was wrong with me, they decided to treat me for typhoid. Some of the symptoms seemed typhoid-like to them, though the tests came negative.

The treatment involved a heavy dosage of antibiotics. This was injected intravenously, once in the morning and once in the evening. Being phobic towards needles did not help my case either. When the antibiotic was injected, I could feel the hot, burning fluid pass through my veins to certain parts of the body. While the liquid would burn my insides, I would scream and shout with pain. Because of the repeated injections they had to keep shifting the location of the intravenous opening (it's the hole they pierce into your body when they have to put you on a drip-like apparatus). All in all, the injections were extremely painful. Antibiotics are rather strong and my experience has taught me, do me more harm than good. They lead to several other complications.

I had seen many people get healed in seconds. But when it happens to one's own self, the feeling of amazement takes one's breath away.

I lost weight, my teeth turned purple, I developed a weird itch in the most inconceivable of places, and loss of hair, loss of appetite, constipation and an array of small issues which, placed together, were driving me insane.

It went on like this for several days. The fever still refused to go down. Once in a while it would graciously dip down to a 102 degrees but never lesser. The fever itself caused a lot of weakness and a host of other problems. I was torturing my body with the antibiotics, yet there was no relief from fever or pain. Visitors and friends had their own 'advice' lined up for me. It was exasperating. Every member of my family was trying to help me, but there was no relief for me.

Finally, when this drama had carried on for too long, Yogi Ashwini intervened. He told my worried mother, "I'll look into it." I was familiar with Yogiji's healing. I had seen many people get healed in seconds. But when it happens to one's own self, the feeling of amazement takes one's breath away. I could hear my mother speaking to Him, on the phone. Just then I wanted to visit the washroom. I came back and felt as if my body was light and comfortable. This felt strange after being in fever continuously for so many days. I called out to my mother. By this time she had just put the phone down after speaking to Yogiji. I told her 'touch me'; she just smiled as she held my wrist.

My fever was 'gone'... Just 'gone'! She almost broke down with relief and gratitude. Within three days I regained my health. No medical science can explain this, yet I know the highest Healer of all, healed me, instantly. It was as simple as that.

Ridhi Kale

24 years, SENIOR CORRESPONDENT, INDIA TODAY

34 the guardian spirit

GURUSPEAK

Rishabh came to me when he was 19, a very regular teenager, who wanted to inquire as to why his mother and sister were wasting time sitting with their eyes closed when they should be having fun? Many people who come to me are here because of a past-life connection with them, something which they have left and their instincts guide them to me. Actually in the present phase of ***kalyug*** *that we are in, we are completing our goals and tasks which we had started in another lifetime. So the majority of interactions are just settling of old scores.*

His first meeting with me told me of our past-life connection. He was a frontline soldier during World War II. I had given him instructions to defend a bunker and not to retreat or abandon it even if he were surrounded. He survived, but I had to leave my body... so instinctively, he just knew that he had to listen to every word that I say and it would save his life and it did... Not just that but it even got him a promotion.

Miracles started happening to me and around me very often from the minute I joined Dhyan Foundation. Initially, it was something unusual but then it became part of my daily life and here I would like to mention some of them.

I recall I had just met Yogi Ashwini, and started my Sanatan Kriya when just a few days later, I went for a movie with my friends at night. After the movie, we were walking towards my car when suddenly I screamed and jumped, pulling my friends with me, just like that, without warning! No one got any time to 'react' or think. As soon as I jumped, I saw a taxi come out of nowhere at a very high speed, and hit the people standing behind me. Some energy had pushed me and my friends to safety. Even till date, the memory of that incident does not fail to astonish my friends. Our lives were saved, and all my friends stand testimony to this miracle.

Once I had to meet Yogi Ashwini and somehow I lost count of time as His presence kept me in a timeless state as if in deep meditation. When I reached my college I realized that I had missed my viva. I thought I would fail but to my surprise, my teacher ended up giving me full marks after a brief talk with me. It was truly amazing!

Before I joined the Foundation, I was frail and weak and used to fall sick very often. But after meeting Yogi Ashwini and doing the *kriya,* I have become much stronger and now I hardly

ever fall sick. My body is now well built and I don't even go for a walk, leave a lifting weights or gymming...I just do my regular *kriya*, and I look and better. It's just astounding that I haven't taken any medicine since I first Yogi Ashwini. It is as if someone has taken complete responsibility for my being!

Rishabh Kale

23 years, SOFTWARE ENGINEER

35 finding my beacon

GURUSPEAK

When Rochak came to me for the first time, I could immediately see the weak energy emitting from the spine. Apparently he looked very tough and muscular but inside he was very weak, without any stamina or actual strength; just a beautiful outer covering of muscles made up of artificial protein supplements.

I knew that in this condition, he would soon end up badly injuring his spine, and his modeling career would be over.

This is a 'typical' and interesting case for the reader because I see this in the majority of young people who come to me. They have very fragile bodies, and are normally into supplements, completely ignoring their proper diets. This leads to an artificial body which is completely devoid of any strength and finally ends up with a serious injury to the spine or the knees. Fortunately for Rochak , he listened to me and gave up the funny diets being prescribed by so called specialists that saved both his spine and him.

I came to the Foundation a few years ago. I was a model by profession. Although I looked well built, my back had completely given way due to over training at the gym. (...though I always hid that fact from everyone.)

I went to meet Yogi Ashwini as I had heard a lot about Him. I saw a well built, strapping man making a bunch of youngsters do some *asanas*. I went up to Him and said, "These are simple exercises, I want to do something rigorous." This handsome, well built and towering figure was actually Yogiji Himself. He laughed and said, "You can't do these simple *asanas* and you are talking about rigorous exercises!" I looked at Him and said, "No-no, you tell me and I will do it." He just asked me to do one simple *asana* and I could not bend. I felt so ashamed. I stood with my eyes downcast. In a gentle, understanding tone, Yogi Ashwini said, "Forget about gymnasiums, just be with me and we'll see." And would you believe it, it has been seven years and I have not been to the gym, and yet now I have a muscular and far stronger body. I don't do any *asanas* anymore and my spine is absolutely in top shape, just like that. It is only my connection with Yogi Ashwini, for there is no other explanation..

When I had come to Dhyan Foundation, I had a speech defect. My speech was not clear. I used to stammer a lot and could not speak in public at all. Yogi Ashwini told me, "Not only will your speech be perfect but you will make presentations/speeches in public fluently". I looked at Him in complete disbelief. But today that is so true. Now with Yogiji's blessings, I give lectures on yog and address crowds! This was a big external change in me. Every one in my social and family circle was astonished; my friends and family are a living testimony to these miracles.

Right after meeting Yogi Ashwini, my first internal experience took place, Yogiji made us sit in *dhyan*. There and then I had a beautiful vision (which I'm not permitted to describe) with my eyes closed. After I got up, I told Yogiji. He nodded and said, "If you connect with the energy, the experience is immediate." On that day I did not fully comprehend what He was saying, but some time later, I just understood.

During *dhyan* I also had an 'out-of-body' experience. I have travelled to various dimensions of existence and come back. Things which were earlier either alien or merely bookish knowledge are now a part of my everyday experiences!

Rochak Bansal

During *dhyan* I also had an 'out-of-body' experience. I have travelled to various dimensions of existence and come back.

28 years, ENTREPRENEUR

36 many roles many goals

GURUSPEAK

It is really very strange to see how our past lives' desires and thoughts manifest in this life. Romi is one such interesting example.

Romi was a princess from Gujarat in India, happily married and surrounded with all riches and pleasures of life. Her husband was a very busy man; as times were changing and royal families were busy doing treaties with the British empire, he was always engrossed in work. She had three very close friends and confidantes with whom she shared all that she was. These three were her support system and major pillars of her life.

*A deep **sadhika,** she would be immersed in meditation for long periods of time but unfortunately, as the grace of the Guru was missing; she could not achieve much in the spiritual world.*

*She had two very strong desires, the first being, that she should be blessed with a Guru and second that before she leaves her body, she should see her three **sakhis** happily married into noble families. Unfortunately, she had to leave her body abruptly and both wishes remained as strong, albeit unfulfilled, thoughts.*

*In this birth, Romi is born in a well to-do staunch Jain family. She is blessed with a devoted husband and three daughters. Her entire life has been revolving around securing her family and looking for suitable matches for her three daughters (her past life **sakhis**). It was only when her daughters grew up and the family was fairly secure that her **anthakarna** opened up and the quest for the Guru started taking form. I say started taking form, because in spite of the fact that her past life **karmas** were so strong, the thought of her **sakhis** overshadowed the desire for the Guru and as we are what we want to be, till she sees her three daughters happily married and settled, she would not be able to enter the domain of the Guru, try as she might.*

*Immediately, as soon as she began the practice of Sanatan Kriya, her past life visions flashed past her and the divine forces began blessing her and revealing themselves to her. But like I said, we are what we want to be, and till our physical desires manifest or we are accepted by a Guru, our thoughts and **maya** do not allow us to go beyond, no matter how hard we try. Our experiences get us the physical but the etheric evades us. Romi is one such perfect example. On an empty stomach, one cannot think about God. One has to first go through the process of satisfaction of the senses and only then, can one go beyond the senses. I always say, '**Bhoga** with the Guru's grace leads to Yoga.'*

I always believed in Divine energy, even as a child I was sure that it is the Divine energy that runs our lives. But my first real encounter with this Divine energy took place, when I met Yogi Ashwini; it was a priceless moment for me. I was transfixed by His presence, tall and powerful yet gentle and protective; His presence touched my very core. Although there was nothing really missing from my life for I had good parents, husband and children, but nothing came to me without effort. My path was full of obstacles. After meeting Yogiji, it seems as if a plate full of material, emotional and spiritual goodies has been kept in front of me. Earlier, I used to make a supreme effort to attain things, now all I want flows towards me effortlessly. It is impossible to put into words, this experience of feeling 'looked after' all the time, in every aspect of my life.

My first definite experience was two days after meeting Yogiji. I was doing *Sanatan Kriya* in my house in the morning, and while doing the 'chant', I smelt roses. There were no roses anywhere; neither in the house, nor outside. It was as if Yogi Ashwini Himself was there and the fragrance was filling the room. It was definitely not the work of an overactive imagination, as I had not been 'told' or tutored on what to expect from the Kriya. I know it happened in real time and space.

A few days later, I was in the kitchen getting dinner ready, and amongst the sounds of the cooker, and the utensils, I heard Yogiji's voice chanting 'OM'. I just froze; I thought it was a figment of my imagination. I ignored it, but once again I heard it, this time even more clearly. I ran out of the

Then I remembered Yogii Ashwini's words, "The first spiritual experiences can come via any of our five senses." I sent a silent salute to this great Yogi.

kitchen to see if the *dhyan* CD was playing. There was no one in the house at that time and no, the CD was not on. Then again I heard the same voice near the dining table 2-3 times. It was an unforgettable experience. My house is fairly spread out, and the other houses are far away so the possibility of hearing this sound from some other physical source was out of question. Then I remembered Yogi Ashwini's words, "The first spiritual experiences can come via any of our five senses." I sent a silent salute to this great Yogi.

After about 3 weeks of starting the Sanatan Kriya, I was doing the '*Panch maha prana dhyan*' sitting amongst all at Bhartiya Vidya Bhavan, when I saw a 'saffron light with the *Gada*', and later I felt as if I was covered with golden light. After the *dhyan*, when I opened my eyes, I saw Lord Hanuman sitting in front of me with his hands folded. Being a staunch Jain it was out of question for me to be seeing such images or deities, I was never told to do such visualisations, then from where and how was I seeing all this? The entire experience defies words and logic, and my heart wells with an immense deep peace every time I recall this incident.

There is no limit to the ecstatic experiences which stem from Yogi Ashwini.

45 years, B.Sc. Homescience, HOMEMAKER

37 it's a dream come true

GURUSPEAK

*Rooble, a very strong pillar of the Dhyan Foundation is a phenomenal storehouse of **prana**. But this **prana** lacked direction, and hence was causing self destruction, within and of the body. She started doing the Sanatan Kriya and also started to participate in the various charity activities of the Foundation. These activities gave an outlet to all the blocked emotions and collected **prana**... So what followed actually was because of her strong faith in the Guru and regular practice. About 'regular practice,' Patanjali, says, "Yoga, **nirantar abhyasa**"*

Yog is a wonderful resource for mankind because it can bring the mind to a state of peace within itself. A global society, which has an addiction to multi-tasking, needs time to "unplug" itself, and Yog offers realistic solutions. This I realized only when I joined Dhyan Foundation.

Ever since I have met Yogi Ashwini, I have experienced quite a transformation in my life.

One profound experience I had when I met Yogiji, which left a deep and lasting impression on me is regarding my daughter.

My daughter was unwell and was diagnosed with tuberculosis by one of the well-known doctors. I was taken aback as the doctor was a known expert in the medical field. But I just wanted Yogi Ashwini to see her once, because it was His opinion that mattered to me the most. On seeing my daughter, He started laughing loudly. I was amazed as to why He was laughing at such a serious issue. He understood my anxiety immediately and said, "Your daughter is absolutely healthy. There is nothing wrong with her". I was extremely happy and a little shocked too. Yogiji asked me to get the tests done again. So I got my daughter's tests done again. These, to my surprise, came out negative this time. The tests proved that she was absolutely fine and had no medical problem. My daughter's life changed in a week. This is testimony to the immense faith that I have in Yogi Ashwini. I know that things can't go wrong if He is there beside us. For a mother, to have such a reassurance for her children is a big thing and I am indebted to Yogi Ashwini for this.

There are innumerable instances of Yogiji's grace. I'm a happy and healthy person today, my pangs of anger have disappeared, and inwardly I feel that I am a much stronger person. Common every day ailments like cough, cold and viral fever have stopped affecting me. Hearing Yogi Ashwini's sermon, one understands the real meaning of life.

Slowly, the negativities of life have started distancing themselves from me. Earlier, I knew yoga, now I have experienced yoga.

In mostly everyone's life, there comes a point when we ask ourselves if we are happy with just being who we are; if we can be something more; if we can grow and explore our full potential; if we can reach some higher plane of existence? Actually, we have read about the higher planes of existence but do we actually believe in them? Do we not think that they are a figment of our imagination? Well, yoga does not tell, but makes us experience these dimensions. There comes a point in life when we all look towards a spiritual path. To me, the only path for awakening the spiritual side and achieving success is through Yogi Ashwini's grace.

I am very thankful to Yogiji for all the blessings. It's difficult to put all my experiences in words but I would like to conclude by giving a quote by Guru Nanak Dev from the holy book Sri Guru Granth Sahib:

"Let no man in the world live in delusion. Without a Guru none can cross over to the other shore. God is one, but He has innumerable forms. He is the Creator of all and He Himself takes the human form that is the Guru."

Roble Sethi

47 years, ENTREPRENEUR

There comes a point in life when we all look towards a spiritual path. To me, the only path for awakening the spiritual side and achieving success is through Yogi Ashwini's grace.

RUCHI KALE REPORT

Brig. (Dr) Ravi Kale

Head of Surgery

Command Hospital

Lucknow

On seeing my wife suffering, I took her to the head of the Gynecology department in the Research & Referral Army Hospital, all tests conducted were negative. Perplexing, all of us, doctors. I then took her to a skin specialist in the Base Hospital, hoping for a solution. She was given heavy medication. Since nothing could be detected, this too failed. After consulting a few of my colleagues I told her to simply bear with it. A few months after she joined the Dhyan Foundation I noticed a big change in her, she did not look stressed and much to my bafflement kept smiling all the time. Slowly it dawned—a miracle had happened. The problem had disappeared and there is no apparent scientific explanation.

September 30th, 2009

Command Hospital CC
Lucknow-1

(रवी काले)
(Ravi Kale)
[illegible]/Brig
ब्रिगेडियर एडम् एवं कमाण्डर ट्रूप्स
Brig Adm & Cdr Tps

38 preservation of the vital

GURUSPEAK

Ruchi, who was a typical high-flying executive, had a very strong energy body, mostly the shades of red and dark green were visible in her aura and ***chakras****. To my surprise, even the* ***shushumna****, which normally should be white or maybe a light shade of blue, was a dark colour; the movement of* ***prana*** *in the* ***ida*** *was negligible, she only had an overactive* ***pingala****, which indicated a very hectic and aggressive lifestyle, so I could guess about her gym workouts.*

Normally, people who have too many interactions have a tendency to develop congestion on the ***surya chakra****, which has the overall effect of slowing down the* ***pranic*** *biorhythm of the* ***pranamaya kosha*** *resulting in excessive weight. The result is that they stick to diets and excessive sweating, which makes the body lose* ***sukra*** *and ageing sets in. They realize the damage once they cross 50, but by then it's too late.*

Luckily, Ruchi started the Sanatan Kriya in time and was able to maintain her ***sukra****. I just balanced her* ***ida*** *and* ***pingala nadis*** *and immediately her* ***pranic*** *flow became normal. Her glow and youthful appearance are primarily due to the fact that she was able to nourish her* ***pranic*** *body with* ***sukra*** *by the practice of correct yoga. Today, I can say with certainty, that she has managed to reduce ageing in her body to a great extent and should look the same for at least the next twenty years.*

As a senior in a leading magazine, I was used to the power my position commanded. Living in Vasant Vihar, with a sound financial background, everything seemed to be at my beck and call.

My evenings were spent in a gym. I was my instructor's star pupil.

Life took a turn when I developed a gynaecological problem, which none of the doctors could resolve. My own husband is a super specialist doctor, hence I had access to all specialists, and yet no cure was available for me. My agony could not be diminished, pain used to come and go at intervals. Even homeopathy and other related alternate sciences failed to provide relief.

A friend told me about Yogi Ashwini. I met him on 22nd Dec 2003. His first words to me were, "Stop going to the gym". My jaw dropped as no one in Dhyan Foundation knew about my lifestyle and habits and it was my first meeting with Him.

I was told to do simple rotations and rest of the Sanatan Kriya. Despite being a gym fanatic, as I was, I failed miserably at my attempts to do these simple rotations. This fact was an eye opener. The gym did not make my body strong and flexible, as I thought it was doing. My first meeting with Yogi Ashwini yielded so much that I was determined to stay and experience more.

I did not talk about my gynaecological problem with anyone at Dhyan Foundation. Nor did I inform Yogiji about it as I felt it was part of my life and I had to bear it. I started Sanatan Kriya practice regularly and attended the weekly sessions with Yogi Ashwini. Three weeks later my husband asked me to show myself to some visiting gynaecologist. It was then, that I was hit by the realization that the problem had disappeared. Just disappeared!

Going inwards was alien to me. But Yogi Ashwini showed the way, and I continued the practice. I was worried that I would put on weight as I had stopped going to the gym. To my amazement I lost five kilos, and my skin had a glow, which drew a lot of positive comments from others.

Emotionally, I calmed down. Earlier, I was like an exclamation mark, but not anymore. My hyper activity is much lower and I am a lot happier. The first vision that I saw was during *Guru vandana.* I saw Lord Shiva in his loin cloth standing tall, right in front ... I was seeing, actually seeing...this colossal form right in front of me! That also when I have never seen such a picture nor was I trying to imagine (daydream) it. And my entire being was filled with inexplicable joy. In my heart I knew Yogi Ashwini was Lord Shiva. I had read about the state of *ananda,* but here I was experiencing it first hand.

I have become a calmer and better person thanks to Yogi Ashwini. I help others naturally and do not feel stressed or tense. Others feel the difference in me and my behaviour.

Ruchi Kale

49 years, HOMEMAKER

39 a story spanning centuries

GURUSPEAK

Ruchi was a court poet of the Mughal dynasty in its prime. Her present husband Mohan was a prince then, perhaps fourth or fifth in line to the throne. I am a little hazy here, but I think it was possibly when Jahangir was ascending the throne.

They were deeply in love and would quite often go on hunts together. I think they were one of those typical lovers, who wanted to share everything, even hunts.

I said I am a little hazy, but the image seems like there is chaos. Their hunting party has by accident, shot a saint-like person in the chest and they are desperately trying to revive him. I can see a ***sadhika*** *with him who is crying, and then I think a curse is put. There is too much vibration, I am not sure, but seems like a time period was set on their separation. And when it ended, they were again together as man and wife in this lifetime. As for her husband, he is severely asthmatic and he goes through immense pain and torture when an attack happens... Let's hope that the time period of the* ***rishi's*** *curse gets over, fast.*

When I came to Dhyan Foundation, I was amazed at the energy levels, dedication and motivation of its members. There was a magnetism here that made me come every evening on Tuesday. A feeling of lightness and happiness used to surround me and would be with me for the rest of the week, till it was time to go back again. I did not understand the word charity, till I saw here how everybody is thinking of ways and means to do whatever they can to give back to society and to the Creator... to put whatever they have in a flow, completely following Yogi Ashwini's teachings of selflessness. Today, I feel a part of Dhyan Foundation. What this means to me is impossible to describe in words.

'*Yoga*' the word till four years back only meant an alternative to exercise and gym workouts to me. One day, lead by a friend of mine, I went to attend a talk by Yogi Ashwini, listening to Him and just looking at Him. I was spellbound by His persona, by His simple way of talking and explaining things. I started coming to the Foundation; that lead to one revelation after another. Everything was an 'experience' and theory had no place. I felt strong, emotionally stable and more with myself by just being in Yogiji's presence. Now, I feel the same even when I connect with the 'Guru' on the etheric level. Yogiji's image is all around me. I find myself merging into Him and the differences just melt away.

I wanted to get married to a boy from a different religion and was facing opposition from my family. I told Yogi Ashwini that it's been six-seven years, and I have decided to marry him without my parents' consent. Yogi Ashwini said to me, "If you want to get married, do so. The whole Foundation is with you. But if you can, then wait for a few days". I told Mohan that we will wait for some days. That very evening, my father came around and within a month, I was married in the presence of my entire family, with my Guru's blessings.

Once there was an acute pain in one of my arms. It was unbearable. Yogi Ashwini told me to look at His finger for some time and asked me to tell Him in three days. Obviously, the pain had disappeared by the next day itself.

Due to biopsy done on one of my knees, they had become weak. I could not hold a position for long. But since I started the *kriya, t*he strength and flexibility in my knees increased. Now I am able to do *asanas* and sit in *dhyan,* and the pain has just disappeared.

After my marriage, I could not continue with my *kriya*. Around that time, pain started in my abdomen. It used to occur sometimes, and was followed by some other physical complications. I showed it to a doctor who diagnosed fibroids. Sometime after these tests, I resumed my *kriya* and met Yogiji once again. I confided in *H*im. He looked at me and said, "Don't worry". My pain and other related problems just went away. Just like that!

I never really visited any temples or any religious places. Now, I know why, because to access the Divine, I just connect to Yogi Ashwini and I see Lord Shiva.

I never really visited any temples or any religious places. Now, I know why, because to access the Divine, I just connect to Yogi Ashwini and I see Lord Shiva right there in *H*is form. So many times in *dhyan*, visions and images of *Shiv, Trishul, Shivling, Sheshnag* are recurrent and the image of Yogiji is one. Now, when I do my *Guru Vandana* and connect with my Guru, Yogiji in *Sheshnag* is present all around. In my *dhyan,* once I had a vision, (a vision when I wasn't being asked to visualise anything nor had I given any autosuggestion to my brain. The visions just came!) that there is a session going on at Sri Aurbindo Ashram with a lot of people in attendance, with Yogiji in the centre. And then Yogiji's form changed to *Sheshnag,* protecting everyone there. And instantly, blue and purple appeared around everyone. This vision has left me mesmerized. I also feel blessed that my Guru's real form has been revealed to me.

RUCHI SINGH REPORT

एक्स-रे रजिस्टर सं॰
X-Ray Register No.

U/s - Pelvis

एक्स-रे रिपोर्ट
X-RAY REPORT

- B/L ovaries (N) size shows multiple follicles
- Small nabothian cyst seen in cervix
- No free fluid
- Uterus normal size anteverted, with endometrial thickness ~ 4mm.
- Two subserosal (exophytic) fibroids seen
Ant wall - 1.2 x 1 cm
Post wall - 2.5 x 1.4 x 2 cm
(No e/o bleed / degenerative changes seen)

ली गई फिल्मों की संख्या व माप
Number and size of films taken

टक्नीशियन
Technician

एक्स-रे विशेषज्ञ
Radiologist

एक्स-रे संख्या व तारीख लिखो
Repeat X-ray No. and Date

तारीख
Date

Imp: Subserosal anterior & posterior wall fibroids.

MGIPMRND—7672/LNH—28.2.2003

S/R

Sometimes, when someone tells me that there is pain or discomfort in some part of the body, I tell them to do something like drink tea, or put oil or ghee in their nostrils with the awareness of my Guru; the trouble ceases to exist or lessens considerably. This is now such a common feature that people around me have stopped being amazed.

Amazingly, questions that come to my mind are answered without even asking by Yogiji in His talks. Mohan and my well-being is in Yogi Ashwini's hands and we fear nothing. We both live a full life under Yogi Ashwini's umbrella of unconditional love.

Ruchi Singh

35 years, FASHION DESIGNER

40 simple living high thinking

GURUSPEAK

Sandeep has been a practitioner of the Sanatan Kriya for nearly three years now, and is a simple man silently walking the path of yoga. It is no surprise that his needs and requirements, no matter how small or insignificant they may sound, are met. The Guru has a constant eye on him; the purity of his practice releases a fragrance which reaches far and wide.

Yogi Ashwini has said many times in His talks, that whatever you give in charity, you yourself will never lack that. Yogiji gave me an experience about one and a half years ago and proved to me, how true each word that Yogi Ashwini speaks is. I feel blessed that I am able to attend the weekly sessions Yogiji conducts for the benefit of people like me.

Under Yogi Ashwini's guidance, I started distributing some eatables like fruits and food to 'not so fortunate' people, who were engaged in construction work. I noticed that at these sites there are women and children also. I started bringing extra food for them too. One day, I was so moved that I used all the money I had in my wallet. After the distribution, I started my motorcycle and drove off to my office. Very close to my office, the petrol needle showed that, the 'reserve' petrol was being used. My heart sank. For a minute the thought crossed my mind that I have no money with me. Next instant, I connected with Yogiji from my *anahat*, and drove to my office. In the office, I soon forgot about my bike and got involved in routine office work.

About mid-day my boss called me to his cabin. I was in for a 'miracle'. My boss handed me an envelope and said, "Here is Rs 3,000, interest on the money you have deposited with me over the last two years". I was stunned. Never in the history of our office had anyone received any 'interest' like this from my boss. Nor had I asked anyone for money. When I walked out of the office my eyes were filled with tears. I could only see Yogi Ashwini all around me. Only Yogiji knew that today my pocket was empty. My heart was beating loudly, and my soul was thanking my Guru. As He knew what to give me, when.

With Yogi Ashwini's blessing, I also started *'sewa'* by teaching math at Dhyan Foundation Anand Vidyalaya, Gurgaon. This has given a new meaning to my life.

Yogi Ashwini has many times talked about detachment, but the concept was not fully clear to me. Once again to make me experience detachment, Yogiji made me go through an experience I would like to share with everyone. I had over the years gotten quite attached to my superior in the office; he was like a mentor, a

brother, a friend.

I was being offered a new job elsewhere, but did not want to go because of my affection for this person. One day I asked my superior, "What if I leave this job?". The answer I got shattered my 'attachment'. He said, "Go, how does it matter to me?" I was shocked and hurt, and in my mind I heard Yogi Ashwini says, "You are alone! The sooner you realize this, the better". Next few days I was there, he was there too, but Yogiji showed me what detachment was. This was a simple incident but it changed my perspective. I keep in mind all that Yogi Ashwini has taught me, as I move forward on this path, and my journey becomes easy. I have realized that we are actually all alone here, and will also leave the world alone. I now experience *'vairagya'* in all my actions. This unique development deep inside me, is a blessing from Yogi Ashwini.

Yogiji says, "You are alone! The sooner you realize this, the better". Next few days I was there, he was there too, but Yogi Ashwini showed me what detachment was.

Sandeep Kaushik

33 years, PHYSICS FACULTY, BANSAL TUTORIAL

41 timeless travel

GURUSPEAK

*Seema! I still remember when she had come to me nearly six years back, referred by a relative who was then an ardent practitioner of the **kriya**. I remember Annu telling me that this lady has tried it all and is very high-headed and might not continue for long. I just said, "Let's see."*

My first meeting with her was very short. I remember this very beautiful lady; she gave me a very big smile (I still wonder about the extent of sarcasm in that, as I was not sure… it seemed to be coming from someone who was saying, "I want to believe it...but my experiences say don't") and she just said, "I don't stick to anything for long. I have been to too many places and you have a maximum of six months to show how good you are."

I just smiled at her and said, "You will have to show me how good you are, only then I can show you how good am I."

Today after six years I see her as one of the main pillars of the Dhyan Foundation. Her dedication to the subject and her reverence did turn out to be extraordinary. She showed me how good she is and of course I had no choice but to show her, how good my Guru is.

To give a brief background about myself, I worked with the Centre for Science and Environment and was with The British High Commission as Senior Public Relations Officer for a long time and my husband is a senior journalist. Coming from such a background, things like 'Miracles' and 'Gurus' were all Greek to me. I was a very practical person, always looking for logic. Being well travelled obviously added to my intellect. Before meeting Yogi Ashwini, I had gone to many spiritual people and various so-called spiritual organizations, but to my disappointment they failed. Let aside strike a chord, they could not even touch a string inside. But ever since I met Yogiji, though initially with lot of skepticism, my search ended and I found my anchor in Him. He made me experience the world which begins where logic ends. My experiences will talk about that mystical world.

My family and I enjoy travelling and being under Yogi Ashwini's grace has made travelling even more amazing. A number of times we have breezed through tricky situations by just remembering Him. At other times, I have been through dangerous circumstances without even realizing it.

Few years back when we were going on a holiday to Austria, I informed Yogi Ashwini and looking straight into my eyes He said, "Be careful, and don't lose control, whatever be the situation." I was puzzled as to why He said this, but in the excitement of going for a holiday I did not bother to ask Him the reason for such a statement. On our holiday, we stopped to visit the Werfen Caves. These are one of the oldest stalagmites and stalactite formations in the caves. The day we reached it was cold and raining with strong winds. We were given special lamps and were told to hold the side rope as the path inside was slippery and treacherous. It is a climb of 134 meters under freezing temperatures and any fall could be fatal. Since we had done a lot of other adventurous stuff, we didn't think much about this warning.

I was okay and I said "Oh! Yogiji held me and got me here". Immediately, I realized there was no sign of Yogiji anywhere.

As we were walking through it, I didn't know when I left the rope. I was holding the lamp in one hand and with the other I was holding my son's hand, who was holding the rope. The others had gone ahead; it was just me and my son trailing the others. Suddenly I slipped; the lamp went out of my hand and I went sliding down. Luckily, my son held on to the rope and screamed. The others were not far ahead and turned back. I desperately tried to find something to arrest my fall but there was just slippery ice. "Yogiji" is all I thought and suddenly I saw Him standing in front of me extending His hand for help. I was not in a state to think what Yogi Ashwini was doing in those caves in Austria when He was actually in India. I held on to Him and slowly edged up and caught the rope. And the next minute I was walking. Everyone came around to check if I was okay and I said "Oh! Yogi Ashwini held me and got me here". Immediately, I realized there was no sign of Yogiji anywhere. His statement suddenly crossed my mind; what He had said to me in Delhi about being careful and not losing control. He knew before I came to Austria that this was going to happen and He saved me. Till date, I can't understand how I saw Yogi Ashwini there in the caves; it can't be my imagination for sure because I remember holding His hand tightly. This is Guru's grace. Amazingly, I did not feel any pain and had not broken any bones. The whole episode must have occurred within a couple of minutes and could have been disastrous; I could have easily broken a few bones or hurt my back. But nothing had happened and I finished the trip without any fuss. At night, when I was changing, I saw an ugly bruise on my left leg, right from the hip joint to my thigh; it was blue but that was all. And even that did not pain.

In one of our other trips we were near a river down South. Everyone was picking thin stones to see how many times we could bounce them on the water. A game we had played often enough. One of my nephews, who was just trying his hand at it for the first time, threw a flat stone but instead of going towards the river the stone slipped out of his hand and flew sideways where I was standing. It came with full force, (my nephew is 6 ft tall and well built) and the stone hit me on my forehead, just above my eye. Just before the stone hit me, I heard Yogi Ashwini saying, "Don't worry nothing will happen". It was a miracle. My eye was saved as the stone was sharp and came at great speed. What is so amazing is that despite its sharpness, it did not even cut my skin even though I could feel the buzz. I just kept rubbing the spot while chanting the *Guru Vandana* within. After some time, when I looked in our car's side mirror, there wasn't even a bruise! It was a close brush again. This time even my husband was surprised about how I survived that.

At another level

Within the first few months of meeting Yogi Ashwini and despite the fact that I wasn't clear about what I was doing and whether I wanted to walk on this path or not, I had the most amazing out of body experience.

My first Diwali, after meeting Yogiji, I was asked do a specific *kriya* at a particular time on Diwali night. During the *kriya,* I heard the sound of OM. Being a cynic, I thought the lady sitting next to me was chanting it aloud but slowly, it dawned on me that it was a very deep male voice and there was no one else around us. In another instance, when Yogi Ashwini took us through a d*hyan session* I saw a jet black *Shivling* amongst the white clouds. I need to tell this, as I was a complete non-believer and would not accept anything which logic could not explain. But how do I explain this! Not once, but twice! When I told Him about it, He just smiled and asked, "So, you still have doubts? You have been given a clear indication." I think He has shown me many times now how good He is.

Do I accept these visions? Well, they were right there and I am still the same person. I have no choice but to accept that miracles happen! These and many other such instances have killed the cynic in me and turned me into a believer.

41 years, HOMEMAKER

Seema Kalra

42 savior & the victim

GURUSPEAK

Shalini has been with me for nearly eight years now, a near perfect practitioner of Sanatan Kriya, someone who has already achieved the state of ***shoonya****. A chartered accountant by profession, she works as a senior manager with Ernst and Young and if she maintains her poise in yog, then by the time this book comes out, I am expecting her to be a partner in her company.*

Shalini's father has been a very successful man in his profession, and had many enemies. This experience can be called a case of direct manifestation of black magic. I am not going into details. All I am allowed to write is that he was attacked by ***sthambhan prayog*** *of a black magician. The day he was attacked, the same day the baby happened to be in the house, hence took the brunt of the force. The mother's vision was of the black force which had been used. And the result was the baby's illness.*

As these black magicians are capable of attacking only the weak, and their energies are also insignificant in the world of ***tantra****. I did not have to do much. A simple reversal of the* ***sthambhan prayog*** *was carried out. And it manifested easily in getting the baby out of the hospital in the prescribed time period. I later inquired and found out that someone close to the family had suddenly fallen very sick; that person was the culprit. Lord Shiva ensured that justice was done.*

There is a lot which a human mind cannot comprehend and understand, since the mind tends to interpret everything with reasoning and rationale. However, there are instances and events in one's life which offer no logical explanation; yet such events leave imprints, which force one to believe that there is a lot beyond the dimension of this physical world. There are forces in the universe that are usable to us. They are there, not to harm or scare us, but to help us evolve.

My sister had just had a baby girl and one night she dreamt that some being in dark clothes is trying to snatch her baby from her. She woke up screaming and sweating profusely in peak January winters and realized that she was muttering "Yogiji, please save my Pavni". Her baby was hale and hearty then. Suddenly a few days after this incident, the baby gradually started becoming weak and pale. When she was just 21 days old, the baby became blue and was rushed to one of the prestigious hospitals in Delhi. The doctors diagnosed renal failure and said that there is just five percent chance of the baby's survival.

I knew that my sister's calling Yogi Ashwini in her dreams was a warning of this unfortunate event. I immediately turned to Yogi Ashwini for help and I knew that only He could save the baby. It was in fact just a matter of informing Yogiji about the health of the baby and from that moment onwards, her condition stabilized and started improving day by day. Sometimes, when I come to think of it, it seems to be a dream, but how can I defy the truth that by merely informing Yogi Ashwini of this tragedy, the matter was taken care of! Yogiji also predicted that the baby would be out of the hospital in three weeks, while the doctors had given her only a five percent chance of survival. Yogi Ashwini told us to get the dialysis machine removed, as according to Him, the baby's kidneys were normal, and did not need the support of the dialysis machine. When we asked the doctors to remove the machine, they thought we had lost our minds to have asked them to do so. They ignored our request.

The amazing thing to be noticed here is that the same dialysis machine, that was being used for the baby, stopped working on its own, and Apollo's paediatric ward did not have a replacement. To the doctor's surprise, the baby's kidneys were functioning on their own without any support. To add to their surprise, as Yogiji had predicted, the kidneys had recovered in less than 10 days. The baby was discharged from the hospital in exactly three weeks. The doctors named the baby a 'Miracle Baby' and accepted and acknowledged that some Divine forces saved this otherwise medically terminal case. Later, one of the major T.V. channels did an investigative story on this case and showcased it in their serial, '*Mano Ya Na Mano*'.

A miracle by Yogi Ashwinis grace, which even the medical experts cannot deny.

Shalini Jain

32 years, SENIOR MANAGER, ERNST & YOUNG

DISCHARGE SUMMARY

NEONATOLOGY UNIT	
Name: PAVNI AGARWAL	Sex: Female
IP No: 82348	ID No: APD1.00511622
Bed No: 3320	
Admission on: 31/1/05	Discharge on:22/02/05

FINAL ACTIVE DIAGNOSIS

Term AGA Newborn
Acute Renal failure
Hypernatremic Seizures
Sepsis
Shock
Pneumonia

BIRTH HISTORY : Baby Pavni, a female neonate, was born to a primigravida mother at term by LSCS (Indication : Oligohydramnios) at Sant Parmanand hospital, New Delhi. No active resuscitation was required, birth wt was 3150 grams and baby was discharged home on breast feeds after four days. She was noticed to pass urine once/twice daily on exclusive breast feeds.

ADMISSION HISTORY : The neonate was admitted at Escorts hospital, Faridabad on 31/1/05 (21 days of life) in a very sick condition. She weighed 2150 grams (lost 1 kg since birth) and was not accepting well orally for 3 days. She also had clonic movements of limbs. On admission she was in shock, severely dehydrated and gasping. She was intubated and ventilation started. The renal parameters showed acute renal failure with very high serum sodium and potassium as well as high blood urea and creatinine. She was transferred to Apollo hospital, New Delhi for further management.

ACUTE RENAL FAILURE, SEIZURES, VENTILATION, PNEUMONIA : At Apollo hospital, ventilation was continued and peritoneal dialysis was started in view of renal failure and gross electrolyte imbalance. Dr Vinay Aggarwal (Pediatric Nephrologist) performed the peritoneal dialysis. Ultrasound KUB showed parenchymal renal disease and renal Doppler study showed poor perfusion with no arterial blood flow during diastole.A repeat renal doppler done after two days showed early diastolic flow to the left kidney.Baby had multifocal seizures during first 48 hrs of stay and were managed with inj phenobarbitone and phenytoin.

ISO 9001 : 2000
ISO 14001 : 1996

Sarita Vihar, Delhi-Mathura Road, New Delhi-110 044, Tel. : 26925801, 26925858 Fax: 91-11-26823629
Emergency No. : 1066

Baby was extubated on 8/2/05 (9th hospital day) and kept on oxygen by headbox. Post extubation CXR showed left pneumonia which was managed with chest physiotherapy and I/v antibiotics. Oxygen was stopped after 5 days.

The renal parameters started improving gradually and urine output started to increase as the dialysis continued. The peritoneal dialysis was continued for 14 days and stopped on 14/2/05 and the urine output remained normal after stopping the dialysis.

SEPSIS :Pending blood cultures,inj cefotaxim was started.Initial blood culture was sterile.On day 4 of admission,in view of falling platelets repeat culture was sent and platelet transfusion given.Inj amikacin was added at 48 hrly dosing.Second blood culture grew Klebsiella and antibiotics were upgraded to inj Meropenem (inj cefotaxim,amikacin stopped).Inj Vancomycin and augmentin were added as a third blood culture sent on day 7 of admission grew coagulase negative staphylococci.Vancomycin was stopped after 3 doses.Inj Meropenem was given for 10 days.

NUTRITION:Tube feeds were started on day 2 of admission and gradually built up to full feeds.Cup and spoon feeds were started on day16 of admission along with breast feeds.Gradually baby was shifted to full oral feeds.

Procedures:Ventilation,Peritoneal dialysis,peripheral arterial line

<u>MOTHER</u>
Age: 30 Years
Primi
Blood group: "O" Positive
Obstetrician: At Sant Parmanand Hospital

<u>DELIVERY</u>:
LSCS (Ind: meconium stained liquor with oligohydramnios)

<u>BABY</u>
DOB:10/01/05 Time:1:35 am
Gestation:term Birth Weight:3150 grams
Apgar Score:
1' --9 /10
5' --9/10

ISO 9001 : 2000
ISO 14001 : 1996

2

43 body building the yoga way

GURUSPEAK

Consciousness permeates through Creation in totality. It is this consciousness from where Creation began and into this shall it merge back. We are also a complete whole of this consciousness, not a part, but the complete whole in totality. The physical body is not us in totality. The Vedic seers in their states of deep ***dhyan*** *saw that they were not just the body, but also something else which was much more powerful and beautiful than the physical. This, they termed as* ***koshas*** *or the subtler dimensions of the human being. Interestingly, they saw that these* ***koshas*** *existed as a separate identity for each individual and, also, as part of one much bigger and more powerful force. They also observed that once these* ***koshas*** *are accessed, then it is possible to carry out any change in one's physical or emotional states with just a thought.*

How can just a thought change everything for us, it is not possible to understand. Also, understanding what I mean to say, when I say that, the human is an individual and also the complete collective, is nearly impossible. Only the experience of Yoga can make one understand, how it is possible! A normal mind cannot comprehend this fact without the grace of the Guru.

Shivan also was a normal mind when he first came to me, a very normal teenager who was wasting his energy and life in the gym and in chasing his girlfriend. Actually, no, I need to correct myself here. It is more appropriate to say that he was wasting his time in the gym, but was utilizing his time perfectly well in chasing his girlfriend for he came to me while chasing her only and never left after that.

He, in a few sessions of the Sanatan Kriya, brought his levels of consciousness to such a state that he was able to completely transform his physical self from a freak to a muscleman within a very short span of time and by doing just as he says, "Sitting with my eyes closed, for half an hour per day".

It has been just a little over a year since I joined the Dhyan Foundation, and quite often I find myself smiling as I reminisce over how far I've come since that first day, when I walked into a dark hall filled with people of all age groups and religions sitting and silently practicing something they called Sanatan Kriya.

Little did I know at the time, that this Sanatan

Kriya practiced under the guidance of Yogi Ashwini would be solely responsible for transforming all aspects of my life.

I was addicted to the gym when I joined Dhyan

Foundation. I would work out for 2 hours every day, as I was hooked on to the idea of being thin and having a good physique, not realizing that I had actually started looking weak and unwell.

The first day I came to the Foundation, all I was told to do was to sit 'still' for 30 minutes with my eyes closed and back absolutely straight. Thinking about all the strenuous exercises I would do at the gym every day for hours together, I found myself passing a sarcastic smile. What could be easier than sitting still for half an hour? I asked myself as I began ....

Thirty minutes later, 'Everything!' was the answer I heard from my own self. The realization of how limited my physical capacity was, dawned upon me. My back and both legs caused me unbearable pain after barely 20 minutes. Confused and embarrassed, I lay down, but this was not the end of my embarrassment.

When I opened my eyes after another 30 minutes or so, the first thing I noticed was a gentleman well into his sixties, literally three times my age, with an erect spine sitting absolutely still. I found it difficult to bat an eyelid as I was amazed at how graceful this gentleman looked.

He was just one of the many practitioners of the Sanatan Kriya, each one having a beautiful glow and a strange attraction.

I never returned to the gym after that day, and started to practice the Sanatan Kriya.

Yogi Ashwini's formulation caused a 'desired' physical change in me. My body changed, muscles toned up as never before and the perfect 'V' started forming.

Presently, whenever I meet anyone, who remembers me as the 'skinny, gym freak', I can't help but enjoy the compliments and the look of amazement in their eyes, when they see the new shape my body has taken. What shocks everyone even more is when I say, "I don't go to any gym or do any exercise anymore. I just sit with my eyes closed".

This science is 16,000 years old and unfailing. It's tried and tested and my *Guru* can show its power and efficacy to anyone who wishes to tread this path.

Shivan Chanana

22 years, CA STUDENT

Yogi Ashwini's formulation caused a 'desired' physical change in me. My body changed, muscles toned up as never before.

44 living in a divine cocoon

GURUSPEAK

*I still remember the first time Simrita had come to see me in my office; a plump girl with practically no glow on her face. I asked her to do a few skips and to my horror she just fainted, right there! Normally I don't encourage people to get into yoga to reduce weight, as I believe that good health and a glowing face is just a byproduct of the practice of Sanatan Kriya. If you are unhealthy, then it's assumed that your vehicle is not fit to carry you to the ultimate destination (**param dham**), so the vehicle has to be healthy and fit if you want to get into yoga. Then why did I encourage her?*

Looking into her past life, I realized that she was the third wife of the Sultan of Turkey (this would be somewhere around 120 years back. If the reader gets a chance to look at some old paintings of the Turkish royal family then you would be surprised at the amazing similarity of her features). Her co-wives were very pretty and she was plump and had no attraction on her face, so she was completely ignored by the family. She had no children and used to pass her time brooding over her ill luck and praying to the Almighty for deliverance. Her father (present) who was the caretaker of the royal palaces, would ensure that she would eat properly and would instruct the maids to take care of her.

Not being able to take the burden of this lonesome life, devoid of her husband's love and not being able to enjoy motherhood, one day she took the ultimate exit route and killed herself.

She roamed the three worlds for nearly a century and then finally when the time was ripe, took this birth. The incident that she mentions, where her form began changing was the time when she had lived out the years in this life as a plump woman (and made up for the years remaining when she had exited in her last life) and the time had come for her to carry on with her journey as a normal person.

Now she is a normal person and would enjoy what she yearned for. I'll wait for the lifetime when she shall awaken to the call of the final frontier and get into yoga and exit this cycle forever.

I was 18 and overweight. This fact was killing me. I stopped looking at myself in the mirror. I was practically eating nothing and was going to the gym regularly. To my horror my weight was not reducing at all. To add to my embarrassment, thrice I fainted in

public because of internal weaknesses. I had given up all hope and was slowly slipping into depression because of my body shape. Everyone in the family was worried. Around that time I met Yogi Ashwini and one day when we were all sitting with Him, out of the blue He said, "Ok, any one person just ask for something." I jumped and before anybody could figure out what Yogiji had said, I shouted, "Yogiji! I want to lose weight." Yogiji smiled and said, "*Bas? Kuch bada maang leti.* (That's it? There's so much more you could've asked for)" I can never forget that day, as it was the end of my helplessness. I never shied away from the mirror after that day. Yogi Ashwini granted my wish and without doing any exercises I got a marvelous figure. If today anyone looks at me, they cannot make out how fat I used to be. I sometimes still pinch myself to reassure myself that such a perfect figure is actually a reality. Thanks to Yogiji, I am through with that horrible phase of my life. It is nothing but a miracle for me, as well as the people who know me.

Now, not only am I in good shape but the body has become healthy and strong too. Once, Yogiji was teaching us about physical strength. He made all the people present stand in a queue. And then He made me stand a little apart from the rest. He said that everyone should come one by one and try to push me. Rochak stepped forward; he is more than six feet tall, and with a muscular build as he was a model in those days. He started pushing me and to his surprise, he could not make me move even an inch. Yogi Ashwini was standing just behind me and laughing. Rochak was surprised why he couldn't move me - someone who is 1/3rd his size and weight. This is the strength of a Guru. I can't explain in words how blessed I feel to be with Yogi Ashwini.

One more indicator of the fact that one is in tune with one's Guru is when not only you, but people related to you also don't remain untouched by His grace. One day my aunt called me, complaining of severe stomach ache. She told me that the pain was so severe that she could not even breathe. After some time while talking to Yogi Ashwini over the phone I casually informed him of my aunt's pain. He was quiet for a minute and then without saying anything continued with the conversation. I called my aunt at night and she told me that her pain had disappeared completely and she was absolutely fine (And it had disappeared exactly at that time when I was talking to Yogiji, because I checked in my call log on my mobile). Just like that!

My experiences have continued ever since I met Yogi Ashwini. Many times I get visions of what's going to happen in future. I have seen images of so many Divine beings whom I had never seen earlier. Now, I have absolutely no reason to not believe in miracles.

Simrita Johar

28 years, JEWELLERY DESIGNER

45 finally fit & happy

GURUSPEAK

*Sudesh has spent a major part of her life in the field of education and child welfare. She has been a principal in her academic career and that also a very strict one, tolerating no nonsense either at work or at home. A very well read person, she encouraged her daughter Nitasha to read the **bani** and not just read but become an authority on it. She knows most of the Indian scriptures like the back of her hand and you name a piece of **gyan** and she will quote the text and the verse; I would call her an intellectual marvel.*

The problem was the last word, "marvel," for marvels are meant for museums and for other people to admire them. For themselves, they are only a bag full of ego that says, "I know it all".

*It is said that the world of the spirit begins where intellect ends. The more we read and learn, the more our brain gets full and the lesser space remains for experience. We are all the time in the world of our knowledge, even when we sit for **dhyan**, and so the senses are not stilled and the experience evades us. We don't do **dhyan**, we daydream.*

*A Guru takes you through this world through the path of **gyan** and **gyan** can only come when you experience. Don't forget that in the Mahabharata, Arjuna had to first see the **Vishva roop** of the Lord, before finally believing that he is actually with the Lord. So, what can be said about mere mortals is that experience is the key which only the Guru holds, not any book. Sudesh is a perfect example of this.*

Bua ji, have you taken your medicine?" asked Preeti. "Oh no Preeti, I think I have not taken it for the last 15 days." My own answer stirred me inside. I thought to myself, I am fine, there is no pain, and I am walking all right (I have had arthritis in my right knee for over thirty years). That day, I felt a deep awakening inside me, and I realized that *Sanatan Kriya* had done its magic. There was no need to fill my body with foreign matter in the form of medicines. Ten months have passed since then. A thirty year old ailment treated by Sanatan Kriya alone is truly a miracle.

Way back in 1972, I started to read the ancient philosophical books which included the Four Vedas. I continued reading the *Upanishads* like *Ish, Ken, Taittraya, Attrey, Chhandogay, Mundak, Mandukay, Kath,* etc. I also read *The*

Gita, Japji Sahib, Bible, Kuran , Patanjali Yog Sutra, Vidur Niti and Chanakya Niti and some Jain Agams. I have been connected with DAV and *Arya Samaj* for 50 years. I performed *havans* as taught by *Arya Samaj* every day since 1972. I always felt that although following the religious traditions of one's family was important, but as an educated person, I should also read all religious books to have a wider perspective on issues of faith.

Since the last four years my daughter Nitasha has been sharing with me some great truths she came to know during the weekly discourses of Yogi Ashwini. I had not read about many of the truths revealed by Yogi Ashwini in any of the books I have mentioned. I never believed in any Guru or felt the need of having one. I was only operating from an intellectual level. I realized that these intellectual readings can give you only a human perspective and nothing beyond.

My understanding of Yogic practices totally changed since I came in contact with members of Dhyan Foundation. I came to know that intellectual and spiritual planes stand apart. Reading does not help integrate these two planes. Practices like a *havan* without any spiritual connection is fruitless. The spiritual plane cannot be understood without the help of a true Guru. This realization came when I turned 70 years. Since childhood, I have been adept at many *asanas* and that is what I took yoga to be. But today when I look back, I feel, I have reached nowhere. I wasted my precious 70 years without getting any *'gyan'*, the regret is deep, but the time has gone.

I have heard dozens of spiritual scholars but none had the kind of clarity Yogi Ashwini has. When I asked Him what all books have you read, His simple answer was, "None completely, maybe a bit of Gita, a few Yog Sutras and not all of Patanjali!" I asked Him how do you know all this? His answer was a 'smile'.

Ten months back, I seriously started the practice of *Sanatan Kriya* which has been designed by Yogi Ashwini Himself. My experiences have been magical with this *kriya*. I learnt to visit every cell of my body and lingered a while longer in the areas of pain, discomfort or ailment. To my astonishment, it worked. If just few months of practice can give me what I have received, I wonder what great *karishma* can take place as I advance in my practice.

If just few months of practice can give me what I have received, I wonder what great '*karishma*' can take place as I advance in my practice.

My brother's wife Sushma, had a severe problem in her spine. She was advised to undergo an operation. Meanwhile she read in the newspaper about a workshop on spine and back problems to be conducted by Yogi Ashwini in Delhi. She came from Ludhiana on 14th May 09 to attend that workshop. Right after the workshop she told me, "*Didi,* I have no pain". Another miracle! Seeing her, I realised, it is not all about physical problems. It is about knowing and understanding the human body at every plane and receiving guidance and correction from the Guru, as per one's own need. And only an evolved being can diagnose correctly and treat with 100% accuracy.

I am at peace with myself. Worldly attachments are not that disturbing. I have in my heart taken Yogi Ashwini as my Guru. I only pray that He accepts me and helps me follow the right path on the journey of the soul towards eternal bliss.

Sudesh Ahlawat

71 yrs, PRINCIPAL-BBKDAV COLLEGE for women (retd.)

SUSHMA JAIN REPORT

Dr. T.N Shadangi
M.S. (Gen. Surg.) M.Ch. (Neuro-Surg.)
Chief Consultant Neurosurgeon
DEEPAK HOSPITAL, LUDHIANA

Formerly Professor & Head Neuro-Surgery
CMC, DMC & OSWAL Hospital, Ludhiana

SATURDAY CLOSED

Dr. Chhaya Shadangi
B.Sc., M.B.B.S., D.G.O
Consultant Gynaecologist & Obstetrician
DEEPAK HOSPITAL, LUDHIANA.

Dated 4.5.009.

Sushma Jain
65 F

Backache 2-3 yrs: radiating to (R) leg - 2 yrs.
Intermittent ↑ on walking: - for 10 yrs.
- always (R) side = . Known Diabetic : controlled
→ Last B.S. - 1.04.009: 120 = FBS.

on Rx:
for HTN.
120/70.
64 kg.

O/E obese. - no motor sensory deficit
- B/MA-J-Absent SLR negative:
= Radiculopathy Diabetic Neuropathy.

MRI = Lumbosacral: multiple disc degeneration
L3 4 L4 5 L5 S1 c̄ canal stenosis:
facetal arthropathy:

Adv Decompression: if medically
fit for surgery.
- already on Nurokind.

⇒ EMG. NCV studies - 'DMCH' -
= To continue anti diabetic: and Anti HTN -

< FBS.
PPS -

[signature]

DEEPAK HOSPITAL
Opp. PAU Gate No 1, Sarabha Nagar
Ludhiana - 141 001
Ph. : 0161-2461738-39, 2454523-24,
2451500, Fax. 91-161-2613424

Residence cum Clinic :
1105, Tagore Nagar, Opp.
Radha Krishan Mandir Ludhiana.
Ph. : (R) 0161-2300343
(Clinic) 2302287, 2070072

Timing for Consultation at Res.
8.00 a.m to 9.00 a.m
5.00 p.m to 7.00 p.m
Sunday : 8. A.M to 12 NOON
SATURDAY CLOSED

46 with the all knowing

GURUSPEAK

Pinki ji belongs to a staunch Sikh family. A very gifted person, she has a phenomenal store of ***prana*** *in her. I just needed to activate her* ***antahkarna*** *and the rest is all history. When she came to me I could immediately make out that her last life was a life of a* ***sewadar*** *and she was carrying the blessings of the Gurus. I still remember her sitting at the* ***samadhi*** *of Shri Aurobindo, where I earlier used to give discourses. She would on and off involve me in dialogues, on the philosophies of the Gurus, and the discussions would range from the interpretations of Kabir's verses to the power and vibrations of Baba Nanak's verses.*

She would normally look at me in amazement and ask how I knew so much about the intricacies of Sikhism and I used to tell her that I have not read any scriptures in detail neither Vedic nor the Granth Sahib... The look of amazement and respect in her eyes would deepen. By now, I am used to this look of amazement in peoples' eyes; I do not blame them as the Grace of the Guru is only for a lucky few.

My first meeting with Yogi Ashwini was an amazing experience in itself. This was in July 2001 at a meditation session at Planet Fitness, Panchsheel.

My quest for a Guru to teach me meditation led me to Yogi Ashwini's class. Being a novice, the experiences I had during this session are still clearly etched in my mind. The amazing colours and images that I saw astonished me. How could I see these things with my eyes closed? They were like photographs, clear and 'real', I just could not fathom. My body was forgotten, I was somewhere else. When Yogiji spoke to me, I was brought back to my physical state with a thud. (Those days Yogiji was very strict in the way He dealt with his students but the discerning could feel the bountiful love he had for all.) Very matter of factly He told me that my *mooladhar chakra* was very big and my husband's spiritual *chakra* was developed. He pointed out that the *mooladhar* was the basic *chakra* for human beings and the spiritual *chakra* was of course the highest. Not understanding all this, I was shocked, as I had always thought that I was more spiritual than my husband.

Over the years I had seen my father really suffer because of an eye condition called glaucoma. My own eyes were showing signs of discomfort. I was really stressed and knowing that diseases are often hereditary, I went for an eye check up. The eye specialist, Dr. Sood feared the worst and put me on a host of medicines and exercises. He also told me they might have to do a laser operation in three months. I was very unhappy about having my eyes operated upon, even with laser. Those days we used to meet Yogi Ashwini in His office, so I rushed to Yogiji's office straight after meeting the doctor. I was anxious and agitated. I told Yogi Ashwini everything. He looked at me across the table, just smiled, and looked deep into my eyes... I kept still. Many minutes passed in this connected silence. When I was about to leave, Yogi Ashwini said, "Go meet the doctor again". I was confused by this directive; nevertheless I visited the doctor the following day. He said, "Your eyes are healthy and fit." There was no need for any medication or laser! This miracle shook me to the very roots of my being. I thanked my luck for making me meet Yogi Ashwini. Dr. Sood, who is a renowned doctor in south Delhi, is a living testimony to this miracle.

In 2004, the lower back pain which I used to experience but had forgotten about, reoccurred. Yogi Ashwini called me to His terrace and told me to do a set of 4-5 *asanas*. I started doing them thinking about a friend of mine who despite practicing these *asanas* still suffered with acute back ache. However, I kept my awareness on Yogiji and continued. He was pacing up and down and at intervals would look at me. Just a few minutes had passed since I started the *asanas* and the pain disappeared like it was never there. With gratitude, I whispered, "Pain has gone." Once again, I was made to experience that it was not the physical *asanas* that had worked but the grace that flowed from Yogi Ashwini. My curiosity got the better of me and gently I asked Yogiji, "If the grace has to flow from you, why do we do the *asanas* which stretch or pain us physically?" I still remember Yogiji had laughed out loud and affectionately said to me, "Pinkiji I need to make you do something or else life would be so easy for you. When you are doing something that gives you pain, at least then you think of me with all intensity." Once again I experienced a miracle first hand. This time I was not surprised, as by now, I had started to understand to some extent, the science of the spirit that Yogi Ashwini is teaching. And in all probability, He is the only one teaching this Divine science today.

What I and thousands of His students have experienced in the last nine years, in the physical and spiritual world is phenomenal. Every single day, amazing things happen which have no logical explanation. The power of thought of Yogiji's students is worth mentioning. They think of something and it happens. I do not have to run from pillar to post to accomplish the daily things in my life. It is literally as though things and people are sent to my doorstep and the Guru Himself is doing everything. Yogiji often says that if you are on the right path, then all doors will open to you and the most difficult situations will pass over. We see this happening at Dhyan Foundation repeatedly every single day.

Yogiji often says that if you are on the right path, then all doors will open to you and the most difficult situations will pass over.

A few months back, one of the Dhyan Foundation members got terrible warts on his feet. The skin specialist advised two courses of treatment; take strong medicines or to get the warts burnt with nitrogen. This member confided in me and my first thought was for Yogiji to please help this person. I knew about the warts but not the position. I spoke to Yogi ji and he asked me to call the person on the phone and ask, "Where are the warts?" There and then I called, and lo and behold, this person tells me they were on his feet but had vanished and his skin was absolutely clear! I still remember the tone of utter amazement of this person on the phone that day. Even now whenever he meets me he talks about this 'miracle'.

About seven months back, we met an evolved being, *Mauni Baba,* who had come from Shirdi. He had been in silence for 30 years. I told him that we were doing *Yog* under the guidance of Yogi Ashwini. Very quickly he scribbled on his slate that what you are doing is PhD. Will be tough to do, but go on. This only went to fortify what I have already written that Yogiji is only one of a kind in this *Kalyug*!

With His grace, I would like to pen down all that I have experienced in a full book.

Sumeet Johar

57 years, HOMEMAKER

47 etheric attraction

GURUSPEAK

Sunanda who is the wife of a senior naval officer was very particular about her health. She was the kind who would pop in pills at the drop of a hat. Actually, what was happening to her was that the pills were popping her, and every day her dependence levels were increasing.

She is an extremely vibrant person and also a psychic, who regularly interacts with spirits of people who have departed; she specifically interacts with the spirits of her parents.

Such people have a very volatile ***surya chakra*** *and are very highly charged at the emotional front. They perceive small worries to be major issues and in the process ruin their bodies; she was an ideal case of this imbalance. Her constant interactions with the spirits and her family worries were taking their toll on her; she was getting increasingly unwell by the day.*

In her case, a little correction of the ***surya chakra*** *had a miraculous effect on her.*

I joined Dhyan Foundation on the 6th of June 2006. Don't be surprised. I'm not maniacal at remembering dates, but certain things are just so impactful that they can't be forgotten.

Very often, I used to suffer from indigestion which would keep me dependent on digestive pills. I met Yogi Ashwini and told Him that I was fed up of what I considered an old age problem. He asked me, "How old are you?" I told Him I was nearing 60. He laughed and said, "Oh! 60 is no age. You are young, don't worry, things will be okay. Don't take digestive pills; you will get habituated to them. I don't think you need those pills." If I tell you that my digestion problem was solved completely from that day onwards, maybe you won't believe me. But I have experienced this miracle and can stand by it. No matter what I ate or drank, I was digesting much faster and with much more ease, finally helping me bid farewell to all the medicines I consumed once and for all.

I had also mentioned to Yogi Ashwini that few years back I had taken a fall and had hurt my left knee, and that, with the help of medicines and physiotherapy, I was completely cured, or so I thought.

The medicines and the physiotherapy had definitely failed to permanently cure the pain in my knee as the problem resurfaced, and this time, I was having problem in walking up and down the stairs. Yogiji said, "Just eat, drink and

be merry. If you have pain again, then tell me." Voila! Problem taken care of instantly! My knees automatically started functioning normally not giving me any pain anymore. These experiences are beyond the comprehension of my logical mind but I can feel the effect of this Divine energy. Every time I have met Yogi Ashwini even with a thought in mind about my problem, I have realized that the problem vanishes. How do you describe these experiences? As miracles?! Of course that is the only logical explanation for them.

I would also like to tell the reader that I am a well read graduate from the batch of 1966 and have a very sane mind; I am in good shape. Well into my 60s, I feel much stronger both mentally and physically than ever before. Thank you for everything Yogi Ashwini.

Sunanda Nag

These experiences are beyond the comprehension of my logical mind but I can feel the effect of this divine energy.

56 years, RETIRED TEACHER

SUNANDA NAG REPORT

From: TANVIR REZA (tanvirreza@hotmail.com)
To: hiraknag@yahoo.co.in
Date: Sunday, 13 September, 2009 9:01:07 PM
Subject: medical certificate

This is to certify that I have been looking after Mrs Nag and I find her in very good health;and, excellent for her age.She should continue the good work she has been doing to stay healthy.

Dr. Tanvir Reza
MBBS (CAL), DTMH (CAL), MRCP (LONDON)
CRITICAL CARE AND CHEST SPECIALIST

9339824988

48 a charitable lifestyle

GURUSPEAK

All that happens in our life is not a coincidence. Very scientifically, all incidents of our life are recorded and evaluated by an energy. Then these 'happenings' are given back to us again, in another form of energy, which manifest time to time during the course of our life. Normally, unless we have a Guru, our thoughts take the shape of these forces and manifest at the given time. And at times, certain thoughts of ours manifest and it amazes us... These are just a few of those thoughts catalyzed by the charitable lifestyle of Tanushree.

Ever since I came under the protection of Yogi Ashwini, there are many new things which have happened in my life. The little desires which I have, manifest within no time. As an example, I just went to Punjab's Dera Radha Swami. There while entering the snack bar, I thought that it's been five years since my younger sister passed away, and I wish I could meet some of her friends. Just then, I met one of her childhood friends, who had been with her in college also! It was an incredible feeling to think something and get it instantly. In the last five years I have been there many times but didn't meet anyone earlier.

Once I came to Bhartiya Vidya Bhawan and that day during *dhyan*, I felt Yogiji's presence, walking around inside the hall. Afterwards when I opened my eyes, I was taken aback to see that in physical Yogi Ashwini had not come there. When I came out of the hall then also, I could feel His energy, His presence.

I have been taking medicine for BP for long but for the last one and a half months the dose has reduced substantially. In fact, if I take the dose I am supposed to take at night, then I experience a headache the next morning. The morning dose is needed on alternate days only. The whole day my body is fine with no difficulty or discomfort.

On Yogi Ashwini's birthday, after meeting Him, when I was back home, there was some kind of heaviness in my head due to all the travelling and interactions with many people. I lay down for half an hour with 'Yogiji's awareness' and my headache disappeared. The same day during *dhyan* in Shakti Nagar I 'saw' Him sitting on the stage in *Sukh asana*. The image was clear. One day, I saw Him in my dream at 5 a.m. in the morning. I gave Him water in a plastic glass after washing it with hot water, and then, I made an egg omelette for Yogi Ashwini. When I woke up the following morning, my heart was filled with reverence and gratitude and this feeling stayed with me for a long time. Although it might sound a little awkward, but the dream was exactly like this ... An unforgettable experience!

DR. AJAY AGGARWAL

M.D. (Med.), DM (Diabetes & Endocrinology)

CONSULTANT DIABETOLOGIST & ENDOCRINOLOGIST

Timings :
MOR. : 8 AM to 10 AM
EVE. : 7 PM to 9 PM
(Daily except Sunday Evening)

Res.-cum-Clinic
39/20, Shakti Nagar,
Delhi - 110 007

Mrs. Tanushree — HT
36y F

Rx

160/110 mmHg

- Tab. Hopace H 5 1 O.D.
- ↓ salt intake / fat intake < 6 gm/d

Ajay
11.4.5

S. creatinine 0.9
Urine (R/M – (n)

TSH
Hb – 11.4
RBS – 96

BY APPOINTMENT ONLY

Phone : 011-27240522 Mobile : 9818691391
E-mail : endocrinologist39@yahoo.co.in

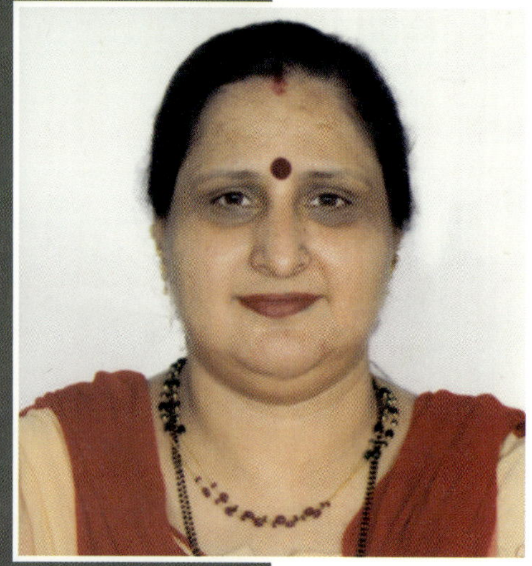

On Sundays, the moment I sit in *dhyan,* my body seems to revolve on its own axis, but when I come out of it, there is no dizziness. Earlier, I used to lose my temper very often. Now if I lose my temper I get an instant headache. As if something in my body is not allowing me to lose my cool. I'm sure all my anger will be gone soon.

Whatever our *karmas,* Yogi Ashwini knows everything about us. I don't feel the need to ask Him questions, but amazingly, whatever questions arise in my mind, they get answered by Him, there itself in His talk and that too with examples! This simply defies logic.

My son's UTI money could not be traced for the last 12 years... We had filed the papers several times but got no response. It was very discouraging. On 4th April, Yogiji's birthday, I had this strong thought that it is high time that the money should be recovered. On 5th April 2009, a miracle happened. We received two cheques in my son's name. We were all surprised as the money had come out of the blue. Instantly, I recalled the previous day and its blessed 'happenings.' I can only thank Yogi Ashwini for His complete sheltering, all the time.

Tanushree

I can only thank Yogi Ashwini for His complete sheltering, all the time.

38 years, HOMEMAKER

49 premonition & safety

GURUSPEAK

*Vaibhav, a brilliant student, but as all those who have something extra-ordinary about them, also have either a hidden energy or a strong volatile trait. He also had a hidden source of phenomenal **pranic** energy in him. The first time I saw him, he was wearing a white **kurta pyjama** and sitting in a corner of the hall, a very shy person, but I could actually feel the radiance from him.*

I knew that he would channelize his hidden potential towards spiritual and material upliftment and would easily succeed in whatever he tried...and I think I was right.

He has gone beyond the expectations of his friends and family but, he is still under-utilizing his potential...let's see what will happen now.

I was in the 12th standard when I first met Yogi Ashwini. At that time I had a lot of personal problems and had left my house and was staying elsewhere. My quarrels with my family had made me extremely bitter and angry towards life.

Then I accompanied my aunt for one *dhyan* session. From then on, I used to attend the sessions regularly. Initially, I used to just sit there, not knowing why I was drawn to these sessions. I hardly got into any conversation with Yogiji. I just made eye contact with Him, but I would still attend. With time, as I practiced *Sanatan Kriya,* I felt myself getting calmer and more 'accepting' of things around me.

When it was time to go to college, I got a little worried. I wondered if I would be able to follow the *kriya* without attending *dhyan* sessions and meeting Yogi Ashwini. I was going to study engineering in Chennai. I knew that I would not be able to travel to Delhi so often. Yogiji assured me that everything would be okay. It was later that I realized that physical distance is of no relevance if you are connected to your Guru.

My initial year in college was really tough, to put it simply. It was a total culture shock, whether it was the people there or the food available. To add to this, I was the only Punjabi guy in that batch and the college was stricter than my school in Delhi. I found it difficult to practice my *kriya* when sharing room space with others who had the usual hostel lifestyle. I had become the butt of all jokes in the college and my batch-mates made fun of my *dhyan* practice. But there was an inner voice, that of Yogi Ashwini, which gave me the emotional strength to continue with my routine.

I turned all my energies towards my studies. I

was anyway the studious type and always did well throughout my school days. This added to my woes, as my excellence in studies also caused a lot of heartburn in others and made it difficult for me to find friends. Though, I was most disturbed by the atmosphere around me but I was also adamant, that I will not break my *niyam*. And then, something amazing happened. Just before the university exams, I started developing a great urge to try drugs. I got very anxious and tried to call Yogi Ashwini, but every time I tried to get in touch with Him (either via email or on phone), I always failed to get through. And then one night, the most unimaginable thing happened. I dreamt the entire Question Paper for my next exam. I wasn't even sure if I was dreaming as what I saw was as clear as crystal that night. At first, I was a bit confused as some of the questions that I saw, were out of the given course. However, because of my unflinching faith in Yogi Ashwini's amazing abilities, I sat in the middle of the night to go through those questions. And lo and behold! The Question Paper turned out to be an exact copy of what I had dreamt the night before. Isn't that amazing?

I knew I had witnessed a miracle. But, why me? I later learnt that it was a warning from the Divine to indicate to me that I was faltering. To my bewilderment, the temptation to dabble with drugs also disappeared overnight! What a relief. I realized that I'm under Yogiji's grace and this was just an indication for me to understand that I was being looked after. It also reinforced the fact that physical distance is of no relevance, if you are connected to your Guru, and as Yogi Ashwini says, "A miracle happens, not to impress you or others around you. It happens because you are faltering somewhere and you have the power to come onto the right path; so a miracle should be the beginning of the journey and not its end."

In another very uncanny instance, I dreamt that I was talking to a guy from my college in the courtyard. After this, I saw that I was washing my face in the bathroom of my house in Delhi, when suddenly my nose started bleeding, followed by bursting of the water geyser, causing my death subsequently. The very next day, to my utter astonishment, I had the same conversation with the same guy at the same spot after dinner. I could not believe that this was actually happening. This left me aghast and I called Yogi Ashwini and told Him exactly what I had dreamt. He advised me, 'not to leave the hostel for the next couple of days'. As luck would have it the very next day, I got the news of my cousins' engagement and was asked to come to Delhi immediately for the ceremony.

I conveyed this news to Yogiji, who told me to travel without any worries. I took the train (sleeper class) from Chennai to Delhi. During the night, our train was stopped and was troubled by Naxals. The ONLY sleeper class coach that was not troubled was mine. While returning, my flight was delayed and was called back from the runway as some technical problem was discovered at the last minute, preventing a major accident from occurring. While some might call these just coincidences, I call it the protection of my Guru.

Ever since my association with Yogi Ashwini, my confidence has grown and I have resolved to face life as it is. I find myself dealing with things much better. After college I even went and stayed in France for further studies; another culture shock, but this time I didn't even flinch.

Vaibhav Kalra

25 years, BUSINESS DEVELOPING ENGINEER,
CONTINENTAL A.G.

During the night, our train was stopped and was troubled by Naxals. The only sleeper class coach that was not troubled was mine.

50 against all odds

GURUSPEAK

The first time I met Vimmy, I immediately knew that she was another one of those victims of the greed of doctors, (not that all doctors are greedy, but like in the field of ayurveda and yoga, we have greedy people, who will just say anything to keep a customer in the lurch), there are people in this honorable profession also for whom money is of prime importance and for that, they will even play with the emotions of a healthy person and would create a fear psychosis.

I believe in the efficacy of modern medicine and at times do take its help also.

This one is a miracle because if a doctor tells you that you are 'dying' and if you refuse to believe it, I call it a miracle. There is nothing much to say here. Vimmy was simply healthy when she came to me and is still healthy. She has a lot of years left in her. All that I did was told her so and she believed me.

When I joined the Foundation I was in a miserable state of mind. My doctor had diagnosed a gynaecological problem; there was a cyst in my ovary, Endometeriosis. All the doctors said that this can turn into cancer. I was scared and dreaded being under the surgeon's scalpel. My doctors embedded the fear so deep into my system, that I became completely negative and morose. My close friends said, 'Don't get the surgery done. It creates hormonal imbalance'. My physical and mental state was in despair. Under these circumstances, I met Yogi Ashwini on the auspicious day of *Gurupurnima*. I just looked into His eyes for help and support. Yogiji looked at me and I felt as if energy was being transferred into my system. He did not say anything, just smiled and His eyes seemed to reassure me. My heart said, 'My cure, my medicine is at His feet alone.'

He told me to sit for *dhyan* that day; I thought to myself, I cannot even sit still for five minutes, how will I sit for the required 45? What will I do? For me, that was the first miracle; I don't know how I sat for *dhyan*, but I did. Soon after this experience, I met Yogi Ashwini alone. That was a unique experience. I felt as if I was alone with a Himalayan *rishi*, saffron clad, wearing *rudraksha malas*, a *tilak* of *bhasm* on His shining forehead, a powerful presence and a caring smile. I felt safe. He listened attentively and said, "Ok, let's see". His aura was so powerful that I felt as if my cyst was cured instantly.

I felt a protection, a cloak of safety encircle me. It was the most amazing, most secure feeling I had felt in many months. An amazing realisation dawned on me a few days later. I got into the routine of my life and 'forgot' about my

I became positive in my thinking and forgiving in my daily life. My entire thought pattern changed.

problem, just simply forgot! I felt fine and healthy. When I realized this, I felt elated and connected to my Guru. Earlier, I was very negative in my thinking. I used to get cancer tests done every two months. After starting my *kriya,* I did not get any test done. My doctor was not at all sure of my behaviour, because I had a family history of cancer. They wanted me to get the 'Ca125' done for cancer detection. I got the test done and to my doctor and husband's amazement, the report turned out to be negative. I was confident of the result even before the test. My tests had to be clear as my body had been trouble-free since the very first day of my meeting Yogi Ashwini.

Yogiji had taken me over the cancer hurdle, that too instantly. I don't feel any discomfort or pain now.

I also slimmed down without any change in diet; I now look like I used to 15 years back. I became positive in my thinking and forgiving in my daily life. My entire thought pattern changed. Actually my entire life changed. I can say that I have realized the true reason for my being here and the purpose of life by Yogi Ashwini's grace.

My thoughts have started manifesting within no time and whatever I think of, happens. One such example is as follows. All my life, I had been dreaming of learning *Punjabi,* to be able to read the *Guru Granth Sahib.* Because of my being with Yogi Ashwini, my thoughts manifested immediately. Soon, I started learning Punjabi from a tutor. Within a month, I started reading the great *Guru Granth Sahib.* A long-awaited wish came true.

Yogi Ashwini has changed my entire life.

Vimmy Chadha

43 years, TEACHER

C-1/B, Clear View, Old DLF Colony, Sector-14, Gurgaon-122001
Tel: 0124 - 2222-253-54/56-57, Fax: 0124 - 2222-258
Main Lab: "Eskay House", 54, Hanuman Road, New Delhi-110001
Customer Service: 011 - 4423-1234, Web: www.lalpathlabs.com

Dr. Arvind Lal
M.B.B.S., D.C.P.
Chief of Laboratory Medicine
FMR HONORARY PHYSICIAN TO THE PRESIDENT OF INDIA

NABL ACCREDITED
M 0058

Dr. Vandana Lal
M.B.B.S., M.D (PATH)
Chief of Pathology
SHIROMANI AWARD WINNER

Name : **MRS. INDERJEET KAUR** **Age** : **42 years** **Sex: F**
Lab. No : **09 9044354** **Referred by:** .
Account Status : **C** **Registered** : **03/04/09**
Report At : **LPL-GURGAON** **Printed** : **03/04/09**

Test Name	Result	Units	Ref. Range
CA 125 @	23.20	U/mL	(< 35.00)

Note: 1. This test is not recommended to screen Ovarian cancer in the general population.
2. False negative / positive results are observed in patients receiving mouse monoclonal antibodies for diagnosis or therapy.
3. Patients with confirmed Ovarian cancer may show normal pre-treatment CA 125 levels. Hence this assay, regardless of level, should not be interpreted as absolute evidence for the presence or absence of malignant disease. The assay value should be used in conjunction with findings from clinical evaluation and other diagnostic procedures.

Clinical Use
* An aid in the management of Ovarian cancer patients
* Monitor the course of disease in patients with Invasive epithelial ovarian cancer
* Detection of residual tumor in patients with Primary epithelial ovarian cancer who have undergone first line therapy

Increased levels
* Primary epithelial ovarian carcinoma
* Healthy individuals (1-2 %)
* First trimester of pregnancy
* During menstrual cycle
* Non malignant conditions - Cirrhosis, Hepatitis, Endometriosis, Ovarian cysts, Pelvic Inflammatory disease
* Non Ovarian malignancies - Cervical, Liver, Pancreatic, Lung, Colon, Stomach, Biliary tract, Uterine, Fallopian tube, Breast and Endometrial carcinoma

Haemoglobin	**10.50**	g/dL	(11.50 - 15.00)

REPORT COMPLETED
Tests Requested:
CA-125 OVARIAN CANCER MAR, HAEMOGLOBIN

Report Validated Electronically.

@ Tests conducted at Main Lab, New Delhi, a CAP (7171001), ISO (FS 60411) and NABL (M 0061) accredited laboratory

51 death laughed at me, i laughed back

GURUSPEAK

The Divine has strange ways of protecting those whose time has not yet come; this was one of those times. When the plastic in the room where there is fire melts, and smoke fills up the air, then its not near impossible but impossible to survive there, specially if you are sleeping through it. Asphyxiation is a certainty, but for those whom the Guru protects, such incidents are like a joke...and like you are amused at a joke, they too are amused.

Life is an incredible blessing of the Lord and when the same Lord took my partner away, I accepted the same and reconciled to my fate. I was left to fend for two small children and I became both their mother and father.

I saw both family and strangers' behaviour and attitude change towards me, which disappointed me on one hand and discouraged me on the other. But, my faith in the Divine has been constant. There were times when I would feel lost, as if searching for some thing; I was unable to comprehend as to what it was that I was seeking. At that stage, my coming in contact with Yogi Ashwini was a strange but very comforting experience. Prior to meeting Him, I would always hesitate and think a lot on all issues, especially before starting any new work or activity, but having met Yogiji, all my confusions and hesitations disappeared.

Now there is no place for fear and disappointment in my life; it has been replaced by positive thoughts and attitude. That's why it is said, that where and when there are blessings of the Guru, the disciple will have experiences of a higher self. I had heard and read this, but now I can say, I have experienced it.

I am a physically handicapped person. In a near-fatal accident, my knee and leg got severely injured, due to which there is a 14 inch long steel rod screwed above the knee. I walk with braces supporting the legs. This pain is now a part of my life. After a long day's work, when I lie down and do *dhyan*, say my *Guru Vandana* and *Shri Maha Mritunjaya Jaap*, sleep comes easily to me. I wake up to the prayer of *Om Namah Shivay*, which fills my heart with bliss and gratitude, I fold my hands and bow in front of the Divine to have given me the right direction and gift of life in the form of Yogi Ashwini.

An incident that happened recently gives me goosebumps when I recall it, and assures me of the Divine hand protecting me and my family.

It was nothing less than Divine intervention that brought my son Amit out of a fire unharmed, safe and cheerful, as if my Guru Himself appeared at the sight of the incident and saved him. It was a miracle for me.

In the month of June, in the early hours of dawn, I was in deep sleep when my son came into the room and slept next to me. The moment he entered, there was a strong stench of fire. When I asked him where the smell was coming from, he said there was a fire in his room and that he had doused it. I was restless to go and see what had happened, as by now I was fully awake.

Outside my room, the smoke made my eyes burn. The smoke had spread from his bedroom into the dining and living rooms. I opened the windows of the kitchen. When I reached the lobby, my eyes started smarting and I started choking as the whole house was filled with smoke. Amit's room was filled with dense, black smoke, which did not let me breathe. I had to come back into the bathroom, wash my face and catch my breath. I tied a wet *dupatta* to my face and entered his room. I opened the windows, disconnected the AC from the plug point and started putting water on the things which were still smoldering. Seeing the smoke come out of the windows, the neighbours came to help. They helped pour water and took the burnt stuff out of the house. The beddings, quilts, bed covers, sheets, mattress rolls, all had caught fire and were slowly smoldering. Their stench filled the house, and it was suffocating. When these things were removed, I was shocked to see that the jute layer below the mattress was still burning and the wooden frame of the bed was charred. Seeing their condition, I realized that these things had been on fire for a long time. The PVC grill of the AC, the synthetic curtains and the thick wires of the AC had all melted out of shape. I just stared at this whole scene, teary eyed.

I turned to look at my son and asked, "The fire has been on for a long time in this room, and you did not even come to know?" He replied, "Yes, mom, I was fast asleep. As the bed had a lot of mattress rolls and quilts on it, I just put a mattress on the floor and went to sleep. The cool blast from the AC was on me, but when I felt 'hot' air touch my body I opened my eyes and saw that the curtains were on fire!"

My son was unharmed in a fire that gutted his room. I have no explanation for a happening like this. Only a Divine being could have protected us like this.

Vinay Talwar

My son was unharmed in a fire that gutted his room. I have no explanation for a happening like this. Only a Divine being could have protected us like this.

70 years, RETD. PRINCIPAL

...and a haunting

entry to the nether world

GURUSPEAK

Arti has lived through a lot, not only has she had experiences of this World, she even has had experiences of That World.

The world of the spirit is very much real, it exists here and now, only some of us have the ability to interact with them and to experience them, but if the spirits choose then anyone can experience them.

If I tell you, you are not alone in your house, what will you say?

Whatever you might say is inconsequential. Just because you cannot see the force of gravity does not mean it does not exist. If you are living on earth then you are bound by gravity. Whether you believe it or not, the world of the spirit is as real as you and I. Arti's narration of this world is backed by her real experiences. The house which she is talking about is still as it was, even after nearly five years of it being sold... You may visit it if you choose to...

As I start recollecting the bizarre and scary events that marred the first twenty-five years of my life, a chill runs down my spine. I start getting goosebumps. It seems like a chapter straight out of a horror movie; a horror movie, which my little niece and me, both have lived through...What I write ahead is not fiction, for it is true—truth sometimes is stranger than fiction.

The time was early nineties. I had just gotten married and was very happy with life. Everything was like a fairy tale—a happy household, stable parents' house, hopes of a bright future ... Suddenly with one phone call everything came crashing down. It seemed like another life, another time. My elder brother, so full of life, was no more. They told me, "He came from work, reported fever and died." Just like that. No illness, nothing. Just gone, forever.

I hastened to my parent's house. There was something eerie about the place, an abominable lull, as if death had not left yet. I was uncomfortable; I had to rush out. It was then that my nightmare began, only to be put an end to by Yogi Ashwini.

My mother started reporting peculiar smells in the house; my little niece would wake up in the middle of the night to strange figures in her room. We could all hear outlandish sounds from the roof, as if furniture was being dragged and soft whimpers.

All of us were petrified. We did not know what to do. Many spiritual healers were consulted. Spirit mediums were called. *Tantrik pujas* were carried out. But all in vain; what is bizarre, had become routine for us.

I remember my mother telling me that this house had been cursed and my father was planning to leave it. Our property was a prime location; being expensive, it was an ordeal to locate a buyer. Time went on...

It was 12th June, 1995. Early morning, the entire family set out for a holiday; my husband and I stayed back. In the evening, the bomb dropped. Their car met with an accident near Udaipur, everyone but my 7 year old niece passed away.

My life collapsed like a pack of cards. My mothers worst fears had come true.

My husband refused to stay with ghosts and spirits. He left and I was served a divorce notice. My niece and I were left all alone to humour our guests from the nether world.

One day at seven in the evening, I heard a scream from the roof. Moments later, my niece came rushing down the stairs, petrified. She had seen a pair of white feet, crooked and turned backwards, walking away! A chill ran down my spine, while researching I had read stories of a certain type of ghost that fits the description! How could my little niece give such a precise description of something that she had not known... It seemed that our guests wanted to get familiar! My niece who is now a scientist, still cannot explain the bizarre sightings she used to have.

Life has a new meaning now. It is beautiful, much more beautiful than I could ever imagine.

I started seeing strange silhouettes and weird faces on closing my eyes. They were so real, as if I could touch them! I developed insomnia and a host of digestive problems, I lost nearly 20 kg and my complexion turned pale. My friends and relatives started saying that I looked like a ghost! Strange sounds were being heard, lights were getting switched off on their own, and I could not tell them what was happening for fear of the word spreading around and my property becoming unsaleable. It became so bad that at a point of time, human visitors stopped coming to my house and my house became one of those haunted houses straight out of a horror movie. The problem was that I could not walk out of this horror show!

My tenants were a famous company, manufacturing and selling greeting cards and gifts. Very shortly they started talking about bizarre happenings, like the cash machine functioning on its own, lights getting switched off on their own. Their staff in a very short span of time started spreading details of the bizarre events to the neighbours. My house and shop became a famous spot for ghost watchers.

One day, my dear friend Shalini took me to a Sanatan Kriya session of Yogi Ashwini. Life took a U-turn.

Yogiji visited my house and immediately asked me to vacate the property. He said that this house was not meant for human residence as someone in the vicinity was directing occult forces here. There was no way of blocking them as any attempt would result in the death of the practitioner. I still remember the day when a *havan* was conducted in my shop and nearly 30 people witnessed a strange white smoke emitting from the corner of the wall enveloping the entire house. Yogiji felt that black magic would prosper there as the spot was one of those rare places from where ghosts enter and exit the nether world. He repeated, "Leave as soon as possible. Till you are here I will ensure that no harm is caused to you. Do not fear, we will not retaliate as it is best to leave this spot for the spirits to reside in."

Within days I could sell the property, that also at a good price and shifted to my new home in south Delhi. I started regaining health, my niece grew up to become a scientist. Life has a new meaning now. It is beautiful, much more beautiful than I could ever imagine. In my new house, once in a while doors do open on their own and lights do get switched off. But this is a joke compared to what I have gone through. When I ask Yogi Ashwini now about this, He just smiles in His mysterious ways. I know why He smiles ... Can you guess?

Arti Gaur

35 years, AYURVEDIC EXPERT

aarti: a form of prayer

Anahat chakra: the chakra situated in the chest cavity, responsible for the functioning of the organs in the chest area. (centre for unconditional love)

ananda: bliss

Antahkarna : the connection with the divine seen in the form a tube of light above the head

Ardhbadh padmotanasana: yogic posture

Arya samaj: a hindu reform movement founded in India by Swami Dayananda in 1875

asana: yogic posture

asato ma sadgamaya ,tamso ma jyotirgamaya, mrityor ma amritamgamya: oh mother goddess lead me from what is untrue to the truth. oh mother goddess from darkness, lead me unto light. oh mother goddess lead me from death to immortality

ashram: hermitages where sages live in peace and tranquility amidst nature

Attrey : a sage who founded the samkhya philosophy; an upanishad

aur batao : tell me more

Ayurveda: medicinal system based on ancient indian texts

bani: voice, as said normally by a guru; set of verses recited by the sikhs

Bargad: banyan tree

bhasm: ash prepared by following a defined procedure for use in yogic practices or as an ingredient in ayurved.

bhogas : gratification of the senses

brahmin: worshipper of brahma, the highest caste in the system of hinduism, and of the priestly order.

chakras: whirling centres of energy in the etheric body, by which the body functions

Chanakya niti: political strategy devised by chanakya, a great scholar of ancient times

Chhandogay: is an upanishad associated with sama veda

darshan: vision

Dera Radha Soami : a centre for spiritual learning at river Beas , Punjab, India

dhyan: state of nothingness

doctor ko dikhao, phir mujhe batana woh kya bolta hai - consult a doctor and then tell me what he says

doctor saab aap toh sach bola karo - doctor, at least you must tell the truth

dupatta: an Indian scarf

ekha tattwa dhyan : meditation on a single element

gada: mace

Ganesh stuti: prayer for lord Ganesha

Gangotri: name of glacier from where the sacred river Ganges originates

Gita: Shrimad Bhagvad Gita, book of knowledge and code of conduct

Gopeshwar: a town in Chamoli district in the state of Uttarakhand, India.

Guru: an energy without which evolution is impossible (vedic thought). a medium between pure divine consciousness and impure being

Guru Granth sahib: the holy scripture of the sikhs

Guru Nanak dev ji: the first of the ten sikh Gurus

Guru purnima: the day of full moon, in the month of Ashadh of the hindu calendar is celebrated as Guru purnima, spiritual Gurus are revered on this day by remembering their life and teachings

Guru sewa: taking the teachings of your Guru forward, aiding his work

Guru shishya parampara: the vedic school of thought wherein a disciple trains under the watchful eyes of the Guru and he/she is monitored every moment. The Guru, being completely responsible for the overall evolution of the disciple, fine tunes the training as per the individual needs.

gurudwara: place of worship for the sikhs

gyan: knowledge which has been experienced

havans: is the term for a sacred purifying ritual in vedic philosophy that involves a fire ceremony.

hiranyagarbha: the golden womb from which creation emerged; the primordial being

Ida: a channel for energy transmission in the etheric body

Ish: an upanishad

Jahangir: was the ruler of the mughal empire from 1605

Jain agams: canonical texts of jainism based on lord Mahavir's teachings.

Japji sahib: appears at the very beginning of the Guru Granth Sahib, the holy book of the sikhs.

kalyug: the last and the present phase of creation

karishma: miracle

karmas: actions

Kath: an upanishad

Ken: an upanishad

koshas : various layers of a being, beyond the physical (levels of existence of a being)

kriya: coded action

kuch bada maang leti: could have asked for something more

kundalini: the force of mother shakti, residing in the base of the Mooladhar chakra

kurta pyjama: Indian dress for men

machan: a vantage point in jungles used for looking far ahead

Mahadev: another way of addressing lord shiva

mahayug: in the vedic timeline it is the grand total of all yugs (an eon)

Mandukay: an upanishad

mantra: codified sound to call upon higher energy that is responsible for a specific function in creation

maya: in vedic philosophy, the illusion of physical reality

moghul: a member of the muslim dynasty that ruled india until 1857.

Mohali: is a city adjacent to Chandigarh, in Punjab, India

Mooladhar chakra: lowest chakra in human beings, in area corresponding to the tip of the tail bone

mudras: the position of the hands or eyes practiced during yogic techniques

Mundak: the head; an upanshiad

Navratra: the word navaratri literally means nine nights in sanskrit, nava meaning nine and ratri meaning nights. during these nine nights and ten days, nine forms of shakti/devi are worshipped

Naxals: or naxalite are a group of far-left radical communists, supportive of maoist political sentiment and ideology.

niyam: discipline as given in patanjali yog sutras

om namah shivay : salutation to lord Shiva

Paanch maha pran dhyan: a step in Sanatan kriya

Padhasta asana: a yogic posture

param dhams: place of pilgrimage in vedic philosphy

pata nahin kal tak to tha ab jaane kahan gaya: don't know, it was there till yesterday, its gone now

Patanjali yogsutra: sage patanjali's (incarnation of sheshnag) treatise on yoga

Pingala: a nadi (channels in the etheric body)

Praan maya kosh: the layer/sheath beyond the annamaya kosh (physical form), which controls the physical

prana: the force in the universe, which makes everything function

pranayams: forms of salutation to prana

pranic: etheric

prashn: question

pujas: prayers

punjabi: belonging to the state of Punjab, India

pursharth : aims of human life

Radha swami ashrams: place of gathering for the radha swami sect

rishi: sage

Rudraksh: evergreen tree (sacred beads of a tree which are used as prayer beads).

Rudraksh mala: prayer beads

sadhika: a woman beginner on the path of spirituality

sadhna: the path to mastery of any form of art, yog, tantra etc.

sakhis: friends

samadhi: an experiential state when in deep meditation

Sanatan kriya: a spiritual evolution technique devised by Yogi Ashwini for the modern person

sandhya: the meeting and parting point between two forces, i.e. the point of transformation. it is that time of the day when the forces which comprise a whole day change from one aspect of theirs into another creating a balance which is most essential for creation

sanidhya : aegis

sardarni: a girl belonging to the sikh community

sewa: selfless service

sewadar: those doing service

shakti: the primordial cosmic energy; mata shakti-mother energy

Sheshnag: one of the primal beings of creation, and according to the Bhagavata purana, an avatar of lord Vishnu

shishya: disciple

Shiva: one of the trinity responsible for transformation

Shivling: lord shiva's form represented in the form of a stone

shoonya: nothingness

Shri Maha mritunjaya jaap: a mantra for lord shiva

Shri Ramkrishna Paramhansa: a famous mystic of 19th-century india

siddhis: boon

sikh: to learn; belonging to, or following the sikh religion

Sri Guru Granth Sahib: religious texts of sikhism

stambhan prayog : an ancient tantrik practice to overcome the enemy (to stop all movement)

Sukh asana: a yogic posture

Sukra: seminal fluid or the lubricating fluid in the physical body

sultan: a ruler of an islamic country

Surya chakra: solar plexus, etheric centre for lower emotions

Sushumna nadi: a nadi (channels in the etheric body)

Taittraya : name of an upanishad, an ancient vedic scripture

tantra: yoga of kalyug, tantra deals primarily with spiritual practices and ritual forms of worship, which aim at liberation from ignorance and rebirth

Tapovan : a place for doing penance

tilak: is a mark worn on the forehead, not to be confused with a bindi

trishul: a trident held by Lord Shiva

Upanishads: ancient vedic text

upayas: a remedy

vairagya: a state of detachment from worldly things

Vedas: oldest sacred texts of ancient india vedic: belong to the time the vedas were written

Veerbhadra: messenger of lord shiva

Vidur niti: a policy followed by vidur a minister in the epic mahabharata

vishva roop: the form of the universe

yoga, nirantar abhyaas: yoga is a continuous practice

Yogi: Title bestowed upon a practisioner of yoga by the Guru.

Yogiji: Title bestowed upon a practisioner of Yoga by the Guru, 'ji' is a symbol of respect in hindi language.

acknowledgements

Mr. M. M. Nambiar
Secretary, Ministry of Civil Aviation

Maj.General B.D. Kale (retd.)

Mr. Prashanto Banerjee
Features Editor, Sunday Indian

Mr. Rahul Chaudhary
Assitant Editor, Business and Economy

Ms. Nitasha Jaini
Visual Artist

Ms. Aarti Gautam
Deputy Commercial Attache'
Consumer & Luxury Goods-Tourism
Economic Mission of New Delhi
Embassy of France

Ms. Ruchi Kale
Homemaker

Ms. Gurdev Kaur
Student

Ms. Chandni Jain
Fashion Designer